Religion at Play

Religion at Play

A MANIFESTO

André Droogers

CASCADE *Books* · Eugene, Oregon

Cascade Books
An Imprint of Wipf and Stock Publishers
199 W. 8th Ave., Suite 3
Eugene, OR 97401

www.wipfandstock.com

ISBN 13: 978-1-4982-2247-1

Cataloging-in-Publication data:

Droogers, A. F.

    Religion at play : a manifesto / André Droogers.

    x + 176 p.; 23 cm—Includes bibliographical references and index.

    ISBN 13: 978-1-4982-2247-1

    1. Play—Religious aspects. 2. Power (Social sciences). 3. Anthropology of religion.
I. Title.

BL65.P6 D76 2014

Manufactured in the USA.

Table of Contents

Preface vii

Acknowledgments ix

Introduction: Bordering 1

one. Exploring Religion 13

two. The Handicapped Human Animal 26

three. Explaining Religion 41

four. Powerful Religion 71

five. Playful Religion 92

six. Weighty Questions Reconsidered 120

Conclusion: De-bordering 149

Bibliography 161

Notes to Poems 167

General Index 169

Preface

WHAT HAVE I LEARNED from my lifelong study of religion in three continents? Is there a lesson that is relevant beyond my own field of study or outside academia? More specifically, if religion is a cause of global problems, operating at considerable human cost, can it also help solve these problems and limit the human cost?

My main argument is easily stated: soon after a religion is founded power mechanisms distort its original potential. Playfulness, in my view, is often closer to the religious founders' intentions. Play is religions' principal asset in their contribution to a sustainable world. Unfortunately, religious leaders are rarely aware of this. Someone needs to tell them. That is why I wrote this book.

Playfulness is also the crucial ingredient in my approach. In my writings so far I have followed standard academic norms, addressing my colleagues as readers; I now move beyond what might be termed scholarly style, adding personal experiences together with fiction and poetry. The book ends with a personal letter to the reader—not a common feature of academic work.

Moreover, this book is unlike others in that it is a practical application of the study of religion, a relatively new field. I want to recover what is best in religion, for the good of global society. In order to do this, I show how power interests have ignored the playful origins of religions, thereby subverting the latter from their primary goals. The consequences are frequently tragic.

I am thus very critical of the track record of religions. And yet this is not another atheist book. It addresses believers but also atheists of the Dawkins and Hitchens variety. I unashamedly call on them to look for what they have in common with believers, rather than reiterating the usual litany of contrasts.

I wrote this book with a wide readership in mind. It is intended more as a long essay, or a book-length manifesto, than as a strictly scholarly study of power and play in religion. That can be found in my other publications. Please enroll in my course in religious playfulness!

Acknowledgments

I GRATEFULLY ACKNOWLEDGE THE editorial assistance of Dr. Angela Argent. I am also indebted to my wife, Ineke Zoutewelle, who is my support and always my first critical reviewer.

Introduction

B O R D E R I N G

Weighty Questions Ignored

RELIGIOUS TURMOIL IS PART and parcel of our days. Samuel P. Huntington[1] suggested that religion would be the main impetus for the clash of civilizations in the twenty-first century. He lived to see airplanes hijacked and flown into skyscrapers. Religious terrorism has become a major political issue globally. Based on religious motives, believers of one religion kill those of another religion. In some regions they thus continue with what their ancestors have been doing on and off for centuries. In other cases believers' violence is new, directed against modernization and the unprecedented radical transformation of global society, yet using ultra-modern means. All these examples are extreme illustrations of the influence of "bordering" religions, their dualistic worldview, and the human cost of that worldview.

Some clarification of definitions is needed. "Bordering"[2] can be defined as *the tendency to treat the results of a group's or a category's meaning-making activities as exclusive and self-evident*. Bordering worldviews stimulate this tendency. The bordering process comprises all that is done to establish and maintain the exclusivity and self-sufficiency of a group's meaning-making. Borders are the social constructs that result from the bordering process. Bordering is not a static, but rather a dynamic process, subject to articulation and criticism. The term worldview refers to religions, but also to secular life philosophies such as ideologies, humanism, and atheism.

---

1. Huntington, *Clash of Civilizations.*
2. Hereafter without inverted commas.

1

I use the term "meaning-making" in a broad sense, referring to the application of the human ability to attach meaning to reality, labeling and interpreting any object, being, act, emotion, experience, person, or relationship, submitting the result itself to new meaning-making, thus combining continuity and change. Meaning-making is sense-making with all the abilities that the human animal has at her or his disposition. Culture and also religion are among the results of collective meaning-making activity. Meaning-making is not just a purely rational, cerebral activity, but may involve emotions and bodily reactions. For example, during the first twenty minutes after waking, I am busy meaning-making, trying to make sense of my strange dream, registering that I feel hungry, deciding what to wear today and why, and responding to my wife's observations. Over breakfast the radio news is aired, the morning newspaper sits on the table, and the world comes crashing in, bombarding us with challenges for new meaning-making. The rest of the day is no different.

There is more to say about the bordering of religions. In their exclusive meaning-making, borders seal "us" off from "them," "insiders" from "outsiders." They separate believers of other faiths from unbelievers. Believers on one side of a border ritually ignore pertinent questions and issues raised by "them." One would think that some arguments and experiences could not be overlooked, and yet in the case of bordering religions they are ignored without a second thought. Believers pay little heed to criticism or challenges from beyond the border. Although in our own era, according to Charles Taylor, religion has become "one human possibility among others,"[3] bordering religions cherish their self-limited claims. Alternative views are ignored, even today, with the unmistakable global presence of religious pluralism. Not even the problem of the unhappy coexistence of religions is able to change this perspective. In fact, the attitudes created at the border may nourish confrontation. In instances where the process of establishing borders leads to splendid isolation, virtually none of the people standing at the border are aware of the censorship that contains them. Not even their leaders, their gatekeepers, seem to be familiar with this mechanism. The question then is how this autocratic process of self-containment comes about and is able to survive in a cultural context that increasingly denies its existence.

The most obvious example of the borders of religion is of course fundamentalism. The term stems from the twelve-volume *Fundamentals*

3. Taylor, *Secular Age*, 3.

published in early twentieth century US Protestantism, but nowadays the phenomenon is recognized in non-Christian religions as well. Fundamentalism has been defined as "a proclamation of reclaimed authority over a sacred tradition which is to be reinstated as an antidote for a society perceived to have strayed from its cultural moorings."[4] In our era, criticisms of the process of modernization (through which science and technology have become important influences in the design of society, culture, worldview, and morals) have become crucial characteristics of fundamentalism.

Yet, the spirit of imagining borders into existence is not limited to fundamentalist religions or to scenarios with human costs. Bordering is an inevitable ingredient of social life. Even tolerant believers employ the "us vs. them" binary schema, sticking by routine or conviction to exclude other views and attitudes. The average believer would never consider moving into another religious group. Any group, whether religious or not, sustains a kind of border control. The sheer existence of a multitude of different groups, even within one tradition, testifies to the importance of religious incompatibility, just as it points to the abundant effects of creativity and imagination. Believers develop their worldview within the spectrum of "us" and "them," with all the possible positions between the extremes, which either polarize, or on the contrary, explore forms of blurring. Inter-religious dialogue proves to be a fraught enterprise, with even conciliatory believers experiencing great difficulty in establishing common ground.[5] In the bordering process, power is a decisive factor, simply because power influences and controls behavior. Though the degree and nature of their power varies, all religious groups, in maintaining their own position, tend to act as powerful religions.

To explore the characteristics of the phenomenon of creating borders and to comprehend the mechanisms behind it, I will start by giving four examples of repressed questions and issues. They include *diversity, the God Debate, power mechanisms,* and *global problems.* Together these show that bordering comes with considerable human cost, both for the believer who builds borders, and for those outside his or her religion. I return to the same examples frequently throughout the course of this book, most explicitly in chapter six. They will help us to reach a better understanding of the bordering process and the *cordon sanitaire* erected around these questions. The discussion of these questions and issues will illustrate that bordering

4. Shupe, "Religious Fundamentalism," 481. Italics in the original.
5. Reedijk, *Roots and Routes.*

3

is not the privilege of fundamentalist religion. I thus seek to find a modus beyond the bordering position. Moreover, I wish to redirect us from the path of powerful to playful religion.

Four Examples

My first example, already touched on, but frequently overlooked, pertains to the *diversity* of religious views that, more than ever before, are visible in the modern world. The mass media now serve as the religions' display window. One would expect that this would cause believers of exclusive religions to worry about the truth of their own beliefs. Unavoidable questions may come to the surface. Should all religions other than my own be considered wrong? Why do other people perceive other things to exist between heaven and earth? Is salvation the exclusive property of my religion? To these and other pertinent and topical questions, "bordered" believers usually turn a deaf ear. They simply continue their daily religious practice, as if there is no problem whatsoever.

Admittedly, theologians of any religion may discuss these topics, but either they affirm the exclusive position, or come up with inventive but ultimately unsatisfactory answers. For example, to give one well-intentioned but widely criticized example, Karl Rahner suggested[6] that all believers outside Christianity are anonymous Christians. It seems problematic to embrace an open attitude towards other religions and at the same time remain convinced that one's own religion is the true one. Bordering deals effectively with this tall order.

Diversity does not only exist in the field of religions, but is also apparent in the contrasts with secular worldviews. Here too, in this, my second example, obvious questions, currently central to the *God Debate*,[7] are often repressed. Believers of bordering religions tend to ignore the challenge of the atheist view, even though it is increasingly claiming presence in public debate. Some believers may enter into a crisis of faith, but the majority is not bothered by the pressing questions that the spokespersons for atheism raise. To these faithful, the God debate is a nothing debate.

The third issue that commonly receives little attention in bordering religious groups is the sociological fact that *power* is an inevitable component of all social relations, including the religious context. Power can

6. Rahner, *Theological Investigations*, 283.

7. Dawkins, *God Delusion*; Hitchens, *God is Not Great*; Hitchens, *The Portable Atheist*.

be defined as *the human capacity to influence other people's behavior, even against their will*. Power is needed to organize any group, since without it the community would be laid to waste by incompatible individual interests. Within religions, power is as present as it is anywhere. The use of violence, a tool often resorted to by those in power or seeking to be in power, is justified religiously, in its most extreme form in contemporary acts of terrorism. Nevertheless, the presence of power in relationships is easily ignored, especially when a religion's core values preach equality or neighborly love and condemn oppression. Power is not a prominent word in religious vocabularies, except when divine power is referred to. Only when a conflict causes upheaval does the distribution of power within or between religious organizations receive attention. Religious diversity may result from power conflicts between factions. But even under harmonious conditions, the question of what the application of power does to a religious group can be raised. Usually this question does not come up, not even in bordering religions, although they present a case in point, since border control requires the active wielding of power.

My final example concerns global problems. The four main *global problems* (i.e., poverty, violence, pollution, and conflict over differences of any kind) often have religious dimensions. Religions may justify these problems in their doctrines and accept them as normal. Admittedly, to varying degrees, religions seek solutions to the four problems and potentially contain the moral justification to do so. Commonly, believers only see their religion's constructive values, convinced that their religion helps solve the current predicament. Rigid borders may render an awareness of a religion's role more difficult. "Other" religions may, for example, be criticized for their disastrous performance in these four problem areas. Yet the question of how a religion can simultaneously be a cause of any of these four problems, and pretend to be able to solve them, is often ignored. How contradictory can believers, and especially their leaders, allow themselves to be? Religions, while causing and legitimating large-scale affliction and conflict, often ignore or deny their complicit role, or point to the role of other factions. Unless the matter becomes breaking news on CNN, the role of religions is not often drawn into question.

The reader may note that these examples seem to nourish a severe critique of religion, and not only in relation to the so-called God Debate. Although some authors writing from an atheist perspective are puzzled by the phenomenon of repressed questions and issues, my book is not another attempt to condemn or repudiate religion. As I will show in this book, religions can be criticized without seeking their extinction. What is more, I suggest that if religious leaders take frequently repressed questions to heart, their religions will have a bright future and will significantly contribute to the wellbeing of humanity. Their religions may even be able to compensate for their anti-human pasts, which attracted rightful atheist criticism. Several anti-religious vindications would then become less pertinent. Terrorism would lose its reason for existence and be reduced to a dark page in the history of religions. In the meantime, we should not forget that there are also a few dark pages in the history of atheism. Moreover, as I will suggest, there is more similarity between religion and atheism than either atheists or believers would care to admit.

Walls

What happens in the bordering process? In all four examples relating to ignored questions and issues, whether the issue is diversity, the God Debate, power, or global problems, bordering religious groups raise walls that protect their own values and meaning-making systems against alternative views. Thanks to the construction of the wall, inconvenient questions can authoritatively be ignored. Although there may be gates and crevices in the wall, the bordering religion fences itself in and its adherents off from what is "out there." The wall is presented as normal, legitimated by seemingly fireproof presuppositions and logic, and often authorized by divine blessing.

Thus a social construct is transformed into a natural *raison d'être*. "We" cannot possibly exist without excluding "them." Most questions about the assumptions of this construct belong to the category of repressed thoughts and are thus silenced. The leadership may have the right to take disciplinary measures against dissenters. Identity consciousness is well developed within such groups, including the tendency to divide the world down dualistic lines, using strong oppositions, such as the line between insiders and outsiders. The message may serve this dualism, to the point that ripples in the edifice must surface. Are these boundaries meant to protect the key message, or does it work the other way around? And is the message formulated in such a way as to legitimate boundary maintenance?

One would surmise that the current process of globalization, the process by which the world is experienced as one place, opens the gates, or at least makes fissures in the border walls that surround religious groups. Globalization might be expected to open out religious enclaves that tend to pose as the one and only site of salvation, the closed world being substituted by the all-encompassing global world. Moreover, as previously mentioned, the process of modernization, defined as the application of the results of science and technology in society, may be expected to make life more rational, threatening the brittle edifice of religious worldviews, by imposing a scientific image of the world. Copernicus, Galileo, and Darwin have played their parts in this transformation. Science and rationality would seem likely to stimulate new questions. Besides, the modern fragmentation of society, an indirect result of modernization, divides people's experience with their world over a number of autonomous contexts, reduces the impact of religious organizations, and exiles them to their own territory. Thus more room for critical views is created.

Yet, globalization, modernization, and fragmentation do not succeed in bringing down the walls of bordering religions, even though they will cause cracks to occur. The inner logic that justifies the bordering view is left intact. Moreover, as is the case with fundamentalism, the reaction to any degradation of the wall may be to reinforce the boundaries, repair the cracks, and secure the gates. Paradoxically, strict religious views, although seemingly pre-modern, represent a cogent recipe to deal with the modern world and are even triggered by it.[8] The prediction contained within the so-called secularization thesis,[9] that religious worldviews will be substituted by rational worldviews, did not come to pass. The problem of repressed questions in bordering religious contexts continues to be as real as it ever was.

One warning is needed as we look for explanations. When we ask how—for heaven's sake—people can ignore obvious questions, the presupposition is that human beings, when reflecting on their world, would follow the rational approach that characterizes science and accept only empirical knowledge as valid. Yet, reflection does not occur in a vacuum. Human meaning-making cannot escape the social and cultural framework.

8. Almond et al., *Rise of Fundamentalisms*; Antoun, *Understanding Fundamentalism*; Lawrence, "From Fundamentalism to Fundamentalisms"; Marty, *Fundamentalisms Observed*; Shupe, "Religious Fundamentalism."

9. Berger et al., *Religious America, Secular Europe?* Casanova, *Public Religions*; Davie, *Sociology of Religion, 46–66*; Davie, *Europe: The Exceptional Case*; Dobbelaere, "The Meaning and Scope of Secularization"; Davie et al., *Predicting Religion*; Hunt, *Religion in Western Society*.

Moreover, human beings are not entirely rational, having other, sometimes contrary, abilities. Bordering therefore occurs more widely than expected. In discussing the matter of ignored questions, this warning should not be forgotten.

From Powerful to Playful

Believers who, in spite of the human cost, ignore questions regarding diversity, truth, the role of power, the atheist critique, and religions' role in the four global problem areas, show the rigidity of the bordering view and the imperviousness of the walls around them. How can we understand this phenomenon? Is there a theoretical and conceptual framework that can be applied to all four examples? Could such an approach offer possible ways to improve the quality of humanity's life, reducing the human cost that bordering religions and other worldviews bring with them?

In what follows, I will explore the potential of an explanatory framework that combines religion, power, and play. Power's part in this approach is obvious, as it prompts a return to one of the four weighty questions just raised. In their exclusivity, bordering religions succeed in directing their adherents' behavior and thus present themselves as powerful religions. Play may be viewed as the surprise guest in this set, but as I will show, it has a crucial role in my approach. Play can be defined as *the human capacity to deal simultaneously and subjunctively with two or more ways of classifying reality;*[10] subjunctively referring to "as if," in contrast with the indicative "as is."[11] From the cradle onwards, play is a basic human capacity. A child plays in spontaneous and natural ways, transforming a stick into a rocket, a doll into a real baby. The same attitude is active in sports and games, when a different reality is established and dealt with temporarily. Play is also practiced when a joke contains *double entendre*. Play always suggests the existence of an alternative perspective. Though this may sound utopian, one consequence of a playful strategy is that believers of bordering religions may be tempted to breach or even demolish the walls around their religion, opening up the opportunity for reflection on alternatives. This statement needs clarification, and seeking to do this is my main aim in writing this book. Let us start with the basics of religion.

10. Droogers, "Methodological Ludism," 53.

11. Turner, *Anthropology of Performance*, 25, 169.

Believers of any religion seek answers to five ultimate questions about any person's individual and social life:[12]

1. why do humans live and die? (the ontological question)

2. what is morally good behavior? (the ethical question)

3. what can be trusted as being true? (the epistemological question)

4. what can be considered beautiful? (the aesthetic question)

5. and therefore, in considering the answers to these questions: who am I, who are we? (the identity question)

So far, religions may seem to present exclusive answers to these questions. My thesis is that in this globalized era, humanity is better served by playful religions, facilitating access to, reflection on, and communication between alternative answers. I seek to redefine religions' role in the world. I trust that, in taking a playful approach, believers, especially in bordering religions, will feel invited to re-contextualize their answers to the five ultimate existential questions. The human cost borne of exclusive religious activity can then be reduced. Those repressed questions regarding diversity, the God debate, power, and global problems can finally be faced.

In developing the playful approach, I will suggest that behavior-directing power mechanisms—rigidly held in bordering religions—tend to restrict the believers' tendency to play with meanings as they seek answers to existential questions. Established power demands unconditional acceptance of unquestionable answers. Those in power are assisted by complacency. Once a limited but satisfactory answer to an existential question is provided, people tend to accept it, despite there being alternative answers available.

Play, when viewed as the human capacity to deal simultaneously with two ways of classifying reality, makes the alternatives apparent. Those in power wish to ignore these alternatives because they threaten their interests. The rehabilitation of play as a religious tool, in combination with the critical surveillance of power as a factor that tends to restrain the playful search for alternatives, will change the process of meaning-making as well as transforming power relations themselves. Symbolic of this transformation, the four examples mentioned above will change. Previously ignored questions regarding diversity, the God debate, religious power, and global

12. Cf. Hijmans and Smaling, "Over de relatie tussen kwalitatief onderzoek en levensbeschouwing," 16–19. See also Droogers and Harskamp, *From Religious Studies to Worldview Studies*.

problem areas, can be raised afresh. Repressed questions become pressing questions. Alternatives can be considered.

This Book

In the first chapter of this book, taking a short story by Gabriel García Márquez, "The Handsomest Drowned Man in the World," as my starting-point, I will explore what religion is about. In chapter two, I will seek to define the human condition, thus exploring the main source from which religion springs. These preparations lead the way into the third chapter, in which, after providing an inventory of the qualities that a theory of religion should contain, I will present my own approach. "Bordering" religions are considered in the light of this theory. In chapter four, I discuss power and the characteristics of a power-driven religion. As an illustration, I begin with a self-authored sequel to Márquez's story. How much room can power come to occupy in a religious situation? How does bordering occur and in what ways are inconvenient questions repressed? In chapter five, I describe the characteristics of a playful religion. In what sense can religion be playful? Chapter six applies what we have discussed so far to the four repressed questions with which I started. How can the move to a playful religion be accomplished? When we go from a religion in which power is all-consuming to a playful religion, how can diversity, the God debate, leadership, and global problems respectively be reconsidered? In relations between religions and secular worldviews, once the playful approach is embraced, common ground can be looked for, instead of the usual contrasts and rivalries. Can religion be made more sustainable, in the service of the world as humanity's place of abode? Should religious education change its framework? And what are the consequences of the playful approach for the study of religion? The conclusion winds up the argument.

The core message of this book is that religion can be perceived in a more playful way. The only condition is that we become aware of the impact that power processes exert on religions. The bordering process, in its violent as well as in its moderate forms, is an expression of how power works and how play is ignored. Religious criticism by atheists focuses predominantly on the abuse of power by gods and believers. In adopting the playful perspective, religion can be viewed from a radically different frame. Power can be shown to work against the primary intentions of the religious *habitus*. Even though power can never be avoided, play, as the serious wielding of a double perspective, is in fact much closer to the source and intention of religion than power itself, including divine power. The fact that religion is scarcely associated with play is an illustration of the icy chill that power structures impose on religions. *Homo Hierarchicus* has sent *Homo Ludens* into exile—from where he must be liberated.

Besides, the playful perspective shows a way out of the digital yes-or-no stalemate that is characteristic of the God Debate trench war. It emphasizes the common elements in theist and atheist worldviews, instead of stereotypical contrasts. The approach through play explores a new theory of religion, beyond antithetical thinking. Moreover, this approach offers a plausible understanding of the differences between religions without taking the tendency to uphold borders as natural, and also—the other extreme— without ending up in global syncretism. The playful view on religion takes the sting out of the God Debate and out of conflicts between believers of different religions.

Though nourished by debates in the study of religion, the applied nature of this book's central argument suggests the need for a type of discourse that deviates from the standard approach in that discipline. My approach is personal and subjective, witnessing to my own path as a believer, a style that is usually frowned upon within the discipline. In writing this book, I sought to go beyond the objective standard style that is thought to be the academic ideal. Each chapter ends with a poem that summarizes part of the chapter's argument in a different manner.

Essentially, this book seeks to change the role that religions and believers play in global society. Believers should learn to wink, playing the religious game in a serious way, taking what is meant seriously, but in a playful way. Peaceful coexistence between believers with different convictions will then become much easier. Standard elements of atheist discourse will evaporate. The most powerful religion will prove to be a playful religion.

As I wend to the shores I know not,
As I list to the dirge, the voices of men and women wreck'd,
As I inhale the impalpable breezes that set in upon me,
As the ocean so mysterious rolls toward me closer and closer,
I too but signify at the utmost a little wash'd-up drift,
A few sands and dead leaves to gather,
Gather, and merge myself as part of the sands and drift.

—*Walt Whitman*

one

Exploring Religion

A Magical Realist Story

In Gabriel García Márquez's short story "The Handsomest Drowned Man in the World,"[1] the children of a fishermen's village on a desert-like cape find the body of a drowned man, a man of abnormal size, washed up on the beach. The children don't know what to do with the giant dead man. All afternoon they play with the corpse, until somebody happens to see what they are doing. The men then carry the body to the nearest house. They wonder why the corpse is so huge. Has the seawater gotten into this man's bones? Did he continue to grow after death?

The men go to surrounding villages to see whether anyone has gone missing. As is the custom, the women take care of the corpse. Once they finish cleaning the man's body, they are left breathless from his beauty and virility. They see that he has borne his death with pride. They keep staring at him, but he simply is too sizable for their imagination. During the vigil that follows, the women grow aware of the tragic irrevocability of his death. Their eyes fill with tears; they go from sighing to wailing and then sing the traditional dirge, improvising new lyrics. When the men return from the other villages with the news that nobody is missing, the women smile in the midst of their tears. "He is ours!" they cry. The men don't see the women's point and wonder what, in their absence, has happened to the women.

1. Márquez, *Collected Stories*, 247–54. The full text can also be found on the internet. Alves, *The Poet, the Warrior, the Prophet*, 23–24, uses the same story but with a different analysis. For the sake of the argument, I have adopted some of the changes Alves introduces in Márquez's story and have also added some elements myself. This section is an adapted version of Droogers, "The Recovery of Perverted Religion," 23–24.

While sewing pants from a piece of sail and a shirt from bridal linen, the women imagine how the drowned giant's life had been, how happy his wife must have been with him, how he had attracted fish by calling them by name, and how springs had begun to flow when he worked on the land. Did he know the secret word that makes a woman pick a flower and put it in her hair? They compare the drowned man with their husbands—who in no way can bear such comparison. This man could do more in one night than their husbands in their whole lives. They thus wander through the maze of their fantasies until the eldest woman, more out of compassion than passion, sighs: "He has the face of someone called Esteban." At dawn they cover his face with a handkerchief, so that the light will not bother him.

Thus the women bring Esteban to life. The men wish to be rid of the dead man. As is the burial custom, the corpse will be thrown off the cliffs. In this village, committing to the earth is committing to the sea. The men tie an old anchor to the body so that it will be gone once and for all. Whereas the men want to return to their normal tasks, the women invent reasons to tarry. They add relics to the bier that the men have made from the remains of a foremast and gaff. The men ask why the stranger deserves decorations worthy of a main altar. But when the women remove the handkerchief from Esteban's face, the men are left breathless too.

Esteban is then given a splendid funeral. Some of the women, who have gone to nearby villages to get flowers for the burial, return with other women, who also feel that something extraordinary is happening. In order not to return Esteban to the sea as an orphan, he is given a father and mother and uncles and aunts from among the best people. He is promoted to kin. Being much more alive than he is, the dead man's splendor is experienced by the villagers as contrasting with their own dullness. In the end, the men remove the anchor so that Esteban will be able to return—if he wishes to do so.

When they throw Esteban's body off the cliffs, they hold their breath for the fraction of centuries—as Márquez puts it—that the corpse needs to reach the sea. They all know that their lives will be different from now on. Henceforth their village is known as Esteban's village.

☙

Though this account is fictional, the case is plausible. It is a modern myth with many pre-modern elements. As I will suggest in more detail in chapter four, when presenting a sequel to this story, we witness the birth of a religious cult that emerges from a mixture of events and experiences, coincidences and strategies, wellbeing and suffering, joy and sadness, Eros and Thanatos, a moment of insight and a hundred years of solitude. Though fiction, Márquez's story could in real life perfectly serve as the founding myth of the Saint Esteban cult. Even a dead body is able to inspire a message of life and hope. To the women, the drowned man belongs to the gray area between death and life. His huge, dead presence interrupts the dull routine of their daily lives. His beauty and virility suggest a possibility of life beyond death. In a waft of sanctity, a cult comes to life. Persons, feelings, events, interpretations, and local customs come together in a constellation that generates creativity and has its own dynamic. The unexpected power of a drowned man is explored by a cult that empowers followers. As we will see, the story shows how people deal with religious experiences, but also how these experiences influence people. This is how religion comes about.

The Margin

Religious creativity flourishes at the margins and in transition zones, in society, in physical space as well as in time.[2] The stories told about the founders of religions or religious movements abound with references to marginality. The founders' marginal—or even marginalized or exiled—position, outside the center of religious power of their time, is emphasized by the reference to deserts, gardens, or caves, and by mentioning transitions in space, such as rivers, or in time, such as midnight, the full moon, or anniversaries. These references may be literally true, but they also come to serve as metaphors. The founders' birth may induce narratives in which margins also appear, for example that the mother is traveling, no longer here, not yet there, as in Buddha's and Jesus' case. During their lifetime, some of the founders roam through the country, without a fixed abode. In addition, in their religion's beliefs and practices, margins may play a major role, such as in rites of transition, meditation, mystical experiences, or pilgrimage. The existential questions that religions seek to answer deal with margins as well, such as between health and sickness, life and death, salvation and loss, and ultimately between the human and the divine spheres.

Let us look again at Márquez's story. As I will show, the children, the beach, the women, and the burial all represent marginality. In the margin,

2. A classical study on margins is Turner, *Ritual Process*. See also Turner and Turner, *Image and Pilgrimage*. On founders of religions, see Droogers, "Symbols of Marginality."

a useful symbolic repertoire lies waiting to be used, expressing the betwixt and between. No rules seem to exist, in contrast to normal human existence, and yet the fullness of existence rules. Márquez makes people play with the endless repertoire of meanings concerning the contrast between the ordinary and the extraordinary, in society as well as in space and time.

Thus the children, with whom the short story begins, are by definition marginal to the adults' society. They do not yet participate fully and are still being trained in the adults' way of life. They are allowed to play, and that is what they do when they find the drowned man. Not yet fully socialized, the children do not understand that one does not play with corpses. They play their extraordinary game, and in their own manner do so seriously, until an adult puts an end to it, imposing society's ordinary course of events on such an extraordinary occurrence.

Once the huge body is carried to the village, the women enter stage. In relation to the men, they are as marginal a social category as the children are to adults. Though women may informally compensate for their marginal position, formally this society appears to be male dominated. Yet the women have their own exclusive gatherings, such as the vigil. Performing the task that tradition ascribes to them in cases of bereavement, they play their autonomous role with regard to the drowned man. Subsequently the men do not understand what has happened to the women. The women even succeed in extending their traditional role so as to temporarily redirect the men's behavior in preparation for Esteban's ritual return to the sea. They invert normal social relations and behave as the mistresses of ceremonies. The men are even left breathless, temporarily sharing in the women's extraordinary experience. The removal of the anchor confirms their faith in this singularly significant man.

Another example of the story's marginal symbolism relates to the location where the drowned giant is found, on the beach, in the margin between land and sea, in the space separating the inhabited village and the uninhabitable sea. The beach is transition zone. Marginalized children play there. The beach also contrasts with the sea. Fishermen risk their lives daily to make their living, inhabiting a space separated from the safe haven of their village. Moreover, the sea is where the dead are buried, offering another contrast with the village of the living. The drowned man on the beach is a reminder of the inevitable passage between life and death. At the end of the story, on the cliffs, the same spatial margin between land and water is emphasized when the corpse is returned to the sea.

Finally, in terms of margins in time, the dead man's burial opens up a short but significant transition period, heralding the birth of a transformed society. Even the nameless dead, washed ashore, can posthumously claim ritual time from the living. Daily life comes to a standstill. Men and women leave their normal duties. For a short period, ritual time becomes more important than economic time. The vigil shifts the usual distinction between day and night. When Esteban's body falls to the sea, people "hold their breath for the fraction of centuries," a double and paradoxical reference to this extraordinary lull in time, short and yet extensive. A heartbeat, like one breath, separates people from their death.

Margins stimulate reflection and ritual action in relation to the ontological, ethical, epistemological, aesthetic, and identity questions mentioned in the Introduction. From there, the normal course of affairs can be looked at from some distance, in a disconnected way. Involvement demands a centered position. Detachment opens room for the consideration of alternatives to the norm, especially when extraordinary events occur, such as the appearance of the drowned man. Playtime lasts as long as the ritual takes.

The Body

The story also highlights the significance of the body in the emergence of a cult. The many layers of meaning contained within the symbolism of the human body invite a playful reflection on existential questions. Like marginal situations, corporality stimulates meaning-making. A focus on the body exists in all religions, even in religions where the soul or the afterlife seem more important.

Almost anything that people can do, using their bodies, has gained a place in religious repertoire. With their bodies, believers perform regular gestures, such as bowing or kneeling. Special clothes cover bodies on ritual occasions. Believers may mutilate their bodies, as with circumcision or flagellation. Experiences of trance are corporeal. The healing of the sick body is an important rite in many religions. Disciplining the body is another common activity, especially when it is perceived in a negative way, as a source of moral inferiority. Meditation practice, fasting, and asceticism put demands on the believer's body. Even the resurrection of the body can be an article of faith. The idea of immortality does away with all the limitations that rule the human body. In beliefs about salvation or enlightenment, the body is an important element. In at least one religion, the body of its founder is eaten, quite literally according to one faction, symbolically in the opinion of the other: "Take and eat, this is my body, given up for you."

In Márquez's story, the body is very present, beginning with the huge corpse of the drowned man, dead but beautiful. Its status as a corpse puts the transition from life to death at the center of reflection. The size and splendor of that body adds to meaning-making. Both men and women invent narratives and statements that describe Esteban's size and allure. Whereas the men seek to describe the corpse's size in a prosaic way, the women are much more poetic. They perform a collective Pieta. From their marginalized position, women, in their search for meaning, appear to be more outspoken and less conditioned than the men in stating their central position. The women explore the exciting implications that the panacea of the giant body opens up and thereby find compensation for the afflictions of their own marginality. The giant body is even said to be too big for the women's imagination. They know that Esteban is as dead as mutton, but against the odds they visualize his life. Through their imagination they bring the dead body to life. They find it necessary to protect his eyes from dawn's harsh light.

The women intuitively reconstruct his life, with an emphasis on characteristics of his body: his size, strength, beauty, and especially his sexual attributes. Since fertility and sexuality mark their identity, they are aware of the role of the body and particularly of their own bodies. It is their body that puts them in a marginal position. As newcomers to the families of their men, the village women share the experience of living with their men's kin group, yet continuing to have their own relatives elsewhere. Their bodies are imported essentially for the continuity of the kin group that their husbands dominate. The bridal linen that they use to make the corpse's shirt reflects their domestic role, just as the piece of sail symbolizes the dangerous profession of the men. In sexual intercourse the women become physically one with their husband, yet in a temporal way. In pregnancy they are one with their child, to be separated after birth. In compensation, their erotic fantasy highlights the contrast between Esteban's extraordinary virility with the poor performances of their husbands. Their laughter is tearful. More than the men they are able to recognize, in a natural way, the marginal characteristics of Esteban's body. As persons occupying the margin, they appear to be the prime architects of the new Esteban cult. Esteban is even promoted to kin, like the women, who were also latently added to the community, however his status is incomparably higher. He is the new icon of the reunited community. An anonymous drowned giant has found a home.

In the theoretical terms set out in the Introduction, the drowned man's body, like the marginal positions discussed in the previous section, stimulates the search for answers to ontological, ethical, epistemological, aesthetic, and identity questions regarding human existence. Matters of life and death, of moral essence, of truth, beauty, and identity are discussed explicitly. The huge, drowned body invites the women to play the religious game. His body is given extraordinary status. Without a trace of proof, miracles are attributed to this man. The women accord him saint-like characteristics. The name that the eldest woman—marginal not only in gender but also by age—gives him, is that of a saint and martyr whose body was sacrificed by stoning.

Symbols

In both Márquez's narrative and the villagers' behavior, the symbol is the main tool for the religious imagination. Symbols serve as models of and for the sacred, representing the sacred and invoking it as well. Together the religions of the world—whether world religions, tribal religions, or religious movements—represent the huge stock of symbols and meanings from which believers from all quarters draw when expressing their experiences with the sacred and finding answers to their existential questions. Extending beyond themselves, symbols are excellent tools to represent and invoke what is invisible, absent, abstract, or belonging to the future—all crucial ingredients of religious messages pertaining to the divine. Thus these characteristics of the sacred can be converted into something visible, present, concrete, and actual. A variety of symbols are brought together, in a more or less coherent way, suggesting connections between them as well as between their respective meanings. Some symbols play a key role, encompassing many layers of meaning, including references to other symbols—as occurs in the Christian Eucharist, symbolized with bread and wine, or in the Hindu wheel of reincarnation. Thanks to symbols, a new way of classifying reality can be explored and played with.

A process of reification occurs, attributing a kind of reality status to what can be thought, even though the thought itself cannot be verified empirically. What can be said via symbolic means, can be thought to exist. Myths and rituals, as symbolic powerhouses, are effective ways of turning the invisible into a real presence. The sacred, made present through myth and ritual, is open to communication and negotiation. Mythical narratives bring with them behavior models as examples for engagement with the sacred, or for appropriate moral conduct. People can identify with the main characters. The stories explain why the world is as it is, on occasion explaining even the reason for the dots on the leopard's skin. In ritual, sacrifice becomes possible. God, the gods, saints, or spirits can be pleased. Their power can be addressed. Believers may share in the ritual, empowered by their religion. Without the human capacity to produce and use symbols, religion would not exist.

In a fictional narrative such as "The Handsomest Drowned Man in the World," symbols are an important tool. Even though the story is written in the style of magical realism, the magical and uncommon are depicted as real and normal. Extraordinary events are described as being plausible. Sober empirical realism is thus amended to accommodate religious and magical features. A drowned man is already exceptional, moreover he is a giant, and as an added bonus, he is beautiful. And yet he is accorded a place in the ordinary village setting. To uncover the religious and magical features hidden within the text, one must delve deeper, through layers of meaning. Ultimately the extraordinary drowned man points to basic existential human questions. Symbols extend beyond themselves. They stand for something that can be better understood through their association with symbol and meanings, just as the women reconsider and come to a better understanding of their lives when confronted with the dead giant. Following from the dynamics of creative reflection and corporeal experience, the use of symbols suggests a movement. Thus, the drowned giant extends beyond himself, at first as the symbol of the uncanny, and only later becoming the symbol of the familiar. Initially he represents death, but is transformed into a symbol of immortality. His arrival alerts the reader to the dangers of the sea, he a victim of the sea, and yet he confers benefit to those who find him. Symbolizing the dangers in life, he comes to represent that which is secure. In the end, and unlike the characters of fairy tales, this giant poses no threat at all. He, and all that he represents, confers a welcome asset to the community. He stands for a better life, a higher quality of existence.

The margin and the body, discussed in previous sections, are important symbols. Whether in society, space, or time, marginality proves to be crucial to the establishment of the Esteban cult, achieved via the meanings given to the body, primarily of the drowned man, but indirectly also by the meanings given to the bodies of the women. The story's realist components infer religious meaning in other ways, such as when the men claim that the bier created by the women's decorations turned Esteban's funeral space into a main altar. There are also potential hidden meanings. That same bier is said to be made from the remains of a foremast and gaff—which could be read as a literal reference to Jesus' cross.

The giant's appearance in the village reforms the religious system. The village is revitalized. Danger is transfigured into blessing. Anonymous foreigner becomes honorary citizen. Posthumously he is depicted as successful, handsome, virile, and loved. Though dead, he establishes his own cult. The puzzling event of the sudden arrival of a giant corpse on the beach is neutralized by the process of meaning-making that it provokes. By accepting Esteban as kin, his appearance is made familiar.

The added bonus conferred by the use of symbols and their interconnected layers of meaning is that some degree of order is established. Symbols convey an order that seems comprehensive. Individual symbols are linked within a consistent worldview with its own dynamics, and these rule the life of the believer. The handsomest drowned man can thus become the mainstay of village identity. He can be promoted to iconic status. His cult reemphasizes the relevance of existing categories in society, space, and time, yet giving them a transformative twist. The social distinctions between children and adults or between men and women are important in the course of events. They are subjected to inversions. As the discoverers of the drowned giant, the children, although immature, play a major role without knowing that they have. Gender relations are temporarily inverted, women taking the leading role in ritual, and turning their skeptical men into believers. Spatial categories that are part of the village classification system are also prominent in the story, dividing the world into the village center, the sea, and the beach, with the cliffs as the vertical equivalent of the beach. Culture and nature, home and work correspond with the contrast between village and sea. As a drowned man, Esteban brings these all together. The time dimension, another component of life, becomes present in a paradoxical way, because it is halted by the discovery of the giant's body. As the villagers deviate from the usual daily rituals, they reconfirm the rhythms of regular time. Conversely, the few seconds during which the corpse falls from the cliff to the sea, are magnified into a fraction of centuries.

In the course of telling Esteban's story, Márquez applies a narrative technique that plays with contrasting symbolic meanings. The villagers move from the negative, mortal world to the positive and resurrected world. A series of inversions takes place. The disheartening inevitability of death is transformed into an encouraging celebration of life. The children's strange and dramatic find becomes a significant turning-point in the adults' village history. The vicissitudes of life are made manageable. The women especially invent fantasies of a better life.

A Sad Personal Experience

As I write this section, on Ascension Day 2012, today as a family we remember a terribly sad event. Five years ago today, on Ascension Day, my grandson Sam arrived stillborn. The pregnancy that sustained him had been normal and full term, and yet, at the very last moment, death intruded before birth. It was a shattering experience for all of us, but especially for our daughter-in-law Annuska. But life continued without pity. That summer we regularly went to Sam's little grave, part of a growing row of children's tombs. More than once an Atalanta butterfly flew around the grave, sometimes even two. During that summer, Sam's brothers, Wouter and Noah, came to spend a few days with us. In our back garden the blackberries were ripe and together we picked them. All of a sudden an Atalanta came flying around us and then settled on the blackberry bush. I got my camera from the house and took a series of pictures. It seemed to me that the Atalanta was quietly posing for me. It was a very special experience.

A year later my wife and I saw the Japanese movie *Still Walking*, directed by Hirokazu Kore-eda. Three generations of a family meet to remember the death of the eldest son Junpei. After a visit to the grave, they find that a yellow butterfly has come into the house, landing on Junpei's picture. His mother immediately interprets this as a sign of Junpei's presence.

A well-known Dutch entertainer, Herman van Veen, had a friend who was soon to die. He asked this friend, in the event that there was life after death, to send him a sign from the afterlife in due course. In order for the proof to be convincing, they agreed that the sign should be as specific as possible. They decided on a butterfly the color of the friend's brown eyes. On the day of his friend's death, Van Veen performed his show, explained that his friend had passed away, and told the audience about the agreement he had entered into with him. At that very moment a brown butterfly landed on him. The audience thought it was part of the show. At the same time the friend's son was also visited by a brown butterfly.[3]

---

3. In one interview (*Algemeen Dagblad*, June 26, 1999) Van Veen used the word "nachtvlinder," literally "night butterfly," or "moth." In another interview (*De Telegraaf*, September 2, 1999), he spoke of a brown butterfly.

How are we to understand such experiences? Of course, I could ignore these examples, by suggesting that statistically speaking coincidences exist and nothing more. I could say that the idea that Sam—or Junpei, or Van Veen's friend—provided a sign from the afterlife is irrational or at least not rational. Dawkins or Hitchens would have used stronger terms. And yet there is an extra component to these events. For example, I could consider it likely, in a playful manner, that Sam's message is "With my brothers I am with you, I am here as well." Junpei's mother and Herman van Veen may well have cherished similar thoughts.

To me the most important conclusion from the butterfly experience is that this symbol of Sam's life, in spite of his death, can be brought into existence. Similarly, the women of the village of the fishermen became free to play with the elements from Esteban's biography. I am able to play with this possibility, regardless of whether it is true or not. I would even be ready to say that the symbolism conferred by the presence of butterflies is probably nonsense, but I find it to be pleasant nonsense. When I see an Atalanta I do not react each time with a devout belief in roaming souls or animated insects, and nor will I lay the foundations for the Society for the Promotion of Belief in Butterflies. I will not do so, even though I know that the butterfly is a forceful symbol. It transforms itself from caterpillar into pupa—seemingly dead—and then is revived as a beautiful butterfly. This confers a nice symbol of the soul and it has been used as such in numerous different cultures. I do not require the institution of belief. And yet, the whole event helped me to cope with Sam's death and birth. Therefore, I will always keep Sam and the butterfly connected. One of the pictures I took of the Atalanta occupies a prominent place in our living room. I play the game seriously, but I understand that I am playing.

I know of one similar event, with a similar conclusion. Sadly one of my PhD students, Ronald Schouten, died of cancer before he could finish his degree. On the day of his burial, half an hour before we were to leave for the ceremony, the pupa of a dragonfly crept up a reed at the border of the small pond in our garden. Going through a number of transformations, a dragonfly came to show itself in all its glory. Again I took up my camera and made a series of pictures recording the stages through which the insect developed into its ultimate form. Then the moment came that we had to leave for Ronald's burial. Hours later, when we returned from the ceremony, the dragonfly, in its final form, was still clinging to the reed. I was able to take one more picture, but then the insect took flight and disappeared. A few days after, my wife went into the garden to fetch something, and when she came into the house again, there was a dragonfly sitting on her back, seemingly the same one that we had seen come to life on the day of Ronald's burial. We could not believe our eyes. I took a picture, and put the insect outside the door. Again, the event is open to meaning-making. We found the presence of the dragonfly comforting after Ronald's tragic death.

I do think that many religions begin with similar extraordinary events, with people smiling inwardly about all the hidden and tentative meanings contained within stories of drowned giants, in butterflies or dragonflies, and in everything else, including our great loss on Ascension Day. The seemingly objective question, imposed on modern wo/man by science and modernization, of whether such a connection is either true or real, ceases to be relevant. The focus is changed. The playful interpretation can be both playful and serious at once, a combination that serious science has difficulty accommodating.

Conclusion

In this chapter we paid an exploratory visit to the field of religion. Márquez's story presents us with a fictitious but plausible situation, in which people are active in the processes of designing and transforming their religious views and practices. People act as meaning-makers, triggered by an extraordinary event. I defined play as the human capacity to deal simultaneously with two or more ways of classifying reality. By playing with possibilities, the fishermen find a new way of classifying reality. The women of the village in particular, are very creative in imagining a new way of classifying the event that in its profane and literal version can be summarized as: "drowned giant washed ashore." Although the arrival of the giant is a serious incident, taken seriously by the fishermen and particularly by their wives, a playful religion is practiced there. The villagers play with symbols and meanings, seeking to make sense of the occurrence. A close reading of the story establishes the importance of margins and the body in acts of religious signification. The Esteban cult is born. The discussion resulting from this shows that believers can be playful, even where life and death seem to intermingle. This also becomes clear from my own sad experience with grandson Sam.

Miracles

Why, who makes much of a miracle?
As to me I know of nothing else but miracles,
Whether I walk the streets of Manhattan,
Or dart my sight over the roofs of houses toward the sky,
Or wade with naked feet along the beach, just in the edge of the water,
Or stand under trees in the woods,
Or talk by day with any one I love, or sleep in the bed at night with any one I love,
Or sit at table at dinner with the rest,
Or look at strangers opposite me riding in the car,
Or watch honey-bees busy around the hive of a summer forenoon,
Or animals feeding in the fields,
Or birds, or the wonderfulness of insects in the air,
Or the wonderfulness of the sun-down, or of stars shining so quiet and bright,
Or the exquisite delicate thin curve of the new moon in spring;
These, with the rest, one and all, are to me miracles,
The whole referring, yet each distinct and in its place.

To me, every hour of the light and dark is a miracle,
Every cubic inch of space is a miracle,
Every square yard of the surface of the earth is spread with the same,
Every foot of the interior swarms with the same.

To me the sea is a continual miracle,
The fishes that swim—the rocks—the motion of the waves—the ships, with men
    in them,
What stranger miracles are there?

—*Walt Whitman*

t w o

The Handicapped Human Animal

From Esteban's Village to the Global Village

THE PEOPLE IN ESTEBAN'S village illustrate how human beings, in a serious but playful way, constantly manipulate and revise their worldview. In the fishermen's village, within twenty-four hours, a classic high drama occurs, beginning with the sudden appearance of a handsome drowned giant, washed up on their beach. The women's choir sings the dirge. The drama results in the creation of a new perspective. The villagers find fresh ways to understand their world and to make sense of the events of their daily life. They deal with things that are both common and unusual, minor questions and the huge existential ones, and discover alternative answers. The revitalized worldview enlarges their repertoire for understanding reality and events—until, some day in the future, a new event will cause new changes. These fishermen and their wives are the authors of the new worldview, but they also are its objects. Under changing circumstances they refashion traditional views. In the process they themselves are changed as well.

The dynamics of the worldview in the fishermen's village translate into a more universal model, as was suggested by my butterfly and dragonfly stories. How can this human capacity for playfulness be understood? The capacity for play seems to be intrinsically part of the human outfit. Consequently we should look at the emergence of the human animal capable of reflection. What place does play, as a universal human capacity, occupy within it? Moreover, now that all human animals inhabit the global village, what is the current role of play?

The Human Condition

Why are human beings playful? To understand this and also to explore the link between play and religion, we have to unravel the human condition. There is one aspect that seems crucial to me. By some quirk of evolution the human brain is equipped with an extraordinary ability to reflect on reality. As has often been shown, this capacity finds no comparison in other animals. Not even other primates, already better qualified in this department than other animals, can compete with the human ape. The first insight into the emergence of the reflecting human animal appears to date from six million years ago, with *Sahelanthropus tchadensis*. However, the real increase in brain volume comes with *Homo erectus*, possibly 1.8 million years ago or slightly more recently. Via *Homo heidelbergensis* and *Homo neanderthalensis*, finally *Homo sapiens* presents himself, probably 2,000 centuries ago, with his real expansion coming 1,400 centuries later.

The human animal is unique in that it differs from other animals in its colossal capacity to make sense of its situation and to do so in a practically unlimited number of ways, experiencing them, weighing them, and considering benefits and costs, and moreover being able to discuss the likely outcome with other humans.[1] It is here that the playful attitude, dealing with more classifications of reality, starts. Even when human beings stick to a more or less fixed way of life, as they generally do, rejecting alternatives along the way, the alternatives that they reject are still being considered. Whereas the other animals have one way of life per species, the human species has as many alternative ways of living as there are cultures in the world. Moreover, in contrast to other animals, humans are able to talk self-consciously about their options.

The diversity in human culture and language does not end there. Within their own culture, human beings do not act as interchangeable clones, but develop idiosyncratic versions of their culture, forming their own unique personalities, deviating from their culture and expressing themselves, if necessary, via a new vocabulary. Language not only serves to *express* views, it also *im*presses opinions, conveying self-determined metaphors that play with the human speaker, just as he or she plays with the metaphors. In sum, unlimited meaning-making of a playful kind, is the exclusive gift of the human being.

1. Cf. Gray, *Strawdogs*, and Safranski, *Das Böse*.

To this picture another element must be added. Being able to reflect on her (or his) own position, considering alternatives, and either rejecting or embracing them, the human animal develops a notion of the self, in contrast with others. This locates any human being in two positions at once. On the one hand she stands apart, being different from the others. And yet, on the other hand, she is social, a herd animal, wishing to be part of larger wholes, of the group in the first place, but also, for example, of the surrounding environment within which she has to find some way to belong. As an individual, a universe unto herself, she is also conscious of the existence of larger wholes within which she must take position. Reflecting on this duality, she can feel both alone and included within those larger collective wholes.[2] In an extreme application of autonomous meaning-making, the lonely human animal, when reaching the conscious decision to put an end to her own life, is the only animal able to set herself utterly and irrevocably apart. As we saw, the women in Esteban's village illustrate the double position of belonging and yet being outsiders, being part of their world and at the same time being set apart. Much of human meaning-making is marked by this duality. Duality also applies to the group, distinguishing itself from other groups, sometimes by violent means, fighting over scarce resources, and yet finding reason to collaborate through marriage and political or economic cooperation. Borders are crossed and ignored, and yet borders are also put in place and defended. This is where bordering begins.

An interesting addition to this prolific tendency towards meaning-making comes from the idea of neoteny,[3] a term taken from zoology, that refers to the retention of juvenile characteristics in an adult animal. In the case of human beings, the term refers to the premature birth of human babies. In comparison with the development milestones reached by other animals at birth, humans should be born after eighteen months of pregnancy.[4] So wo/man is a half-complete product at birth. Culture can be considered to compensate, making up for the shortcomings of the baby human at birth.[5] Culture completes the human outfit. The learning period for humans is prolonged beyond full physical development, bringing hu-

---

2. Baal, *Symbols for Communication*, 219ff. Cf. McGilchrist, *The Master and His Emissary*, 85, 87, 128, 140, 202, 320.

3. Dufour, *On achève bien les hommes*. Cf. Bellah, *Religion in Human Evolution*, 85, 87.

4. Dufour, *On achève bien les hommes*, 41.

5. Ibid., 18.

man juveniles into late adulthood. Incomplete from the start, the adult human animal is malleable, adapting easily to the most diverse situations and habitats. Not made specifically for an exclusive life in a particular habitat, as is the case for most animals, the human animal can survive in a variety of landscapes. The overdeveloped capacity for meaning-making appears to be used to compensate for the neoteny drawback, including the stress that comes with it. Playfulness is part of this human toolkit. Religion has a role to play in this process.

The Rise of the Dragon

The unlimited human capacity for meaning-making, handy as a compensation for premature birth, and completing the semi-manufactured product, has had radical consequences for the human condition. Human history reflects the major and minor changes in ongoing human meaning-making. The agricultural revolution (8,000 to 5,000 B.C.) was a first major change, creating an economic surplus, making sedentary housing viable and stimulating urbanization. The human animal proved to be able to change his way of life drastically. His efforts also resulted in a more complex labor division around city states, including specialized agricultural, artisanal, political, and religious classes. Over a short period, new alternatives were tested and implemented. A huge play with possibilities began, resulting in a new type of society and culture. Religion changed accordingly, by taking part in the transformation, contributing to it, but also reflecting it. The so-called Axial Period, Karl Jaspers' *Achsenzeit*, from 900 to 200 B.C., occurring simultaneously in Greece, Judea, Persia, India, and China, represents the apex of this development.[6] During this time, fundamental insights within philosophy and religion were formulated that remain influential today. In addition, the basis was laid for Judaism, Hinduism, and Buddhism as world religions, and Christianity and Islam came later as elaborations of the Judaic tradition. Interestingly this era has been characterized as an in-between period that allowed much scope for experiments in meaning-making.

But the most transformative applications of human meaning-making came with modernization, starting around 1800, in the wake of the upsurge of meaning-making in science and technology. The consequence was a

6. For a recent overview, see Armstrong, *The Great Transformation*; also Bellah, *Religion in Human Evolution*, chapters 6 to 9. For a novel on that period, see Vidal, *Creation*.

radical restructuring of society, culminating in an unprecedented constellation, both in complexity and scale. The application of the results of science and technology in society led not only to industrialization. Better health care became possible, facilitating unparalleled population growth. Industrial development stimulated labor migration, and also the frantic quest for raw materials, serving as an impetus for colonialism. Technological change brought much faster modes of travel and introduced global telecommunication. Ultimately, in our time, industry and technology transformed the world into one single place, the global village. The introduction of computers was another technological innovation with far-reaching consequences. The majority of the world's population now live in cities, some of them mega-cities. Social control, traditionally affected by kinship, politics, and religion, was eroded. The authentic individual has been put on a pedestal, as a model hero of a new way of life.

Although we all experience changes in our day-to-day activities, we are rarely conscious of the contrast between the extraordinary complex society we are part of and the kind of society that preceded it. The Agricultural Revolution and the Axial Age seem much further away than the number of centuries separating us from these events would suggest. In museums we can admire what we have lost. Even the differences between our own generation and our parents' is rarely ever discussed. Yet even in the short time span between two generations profound changes have occurred, accelerating the rhythm of change.

Nowadays meaning-making appears in its modern form as an ever hungrier monster, a modern dragon, that devours whatever comes within reach of its jaws and that then spits it out again. Modernization applies the results of science and technology in society, with remarkable consequences and at considerable human cost. This dragon has become an object of a global veneration, though some argue that it should be slain, or at least domesticated. Part of the problem is that this monster can only survive in an ever expanding habitat, now extending to the whole world. One consequence of the monster's global presence has been that diversity has increased as a result of hot-tempered meaning-making. Everything that is imaginable seems possible. Inventors enjoy a high status. Paradoxically, at the same time, uniformity has become a requirement of the dragon's system. In the interest of its own survival, it limits the diversity that has accompanied human meaning-making until now. Its cult can only be sustained if its output is standardized. Consumer articles can only be produced with global infrastructure and marketing. Accordingly, uniformity replaces traditional diversity. The same few remaining brands are everywhere around the globe, in the most extreme cases leading to dual options of the Pepsi/Coca Cola or the Microsoft/Apple type. Consumers may think they act as free meaning-makers, but they are ruled by marketing agencies that seem to know everything about consumer behavior. Though we may think that, ideologically speaking, the element of choice has never been so important, materially speaking we are seduced by a limitation of choice that is more pre-modern than modern. The changes that modernization has brought us are complex and contradictory.

The Asset Has Become a Setback

Play is by definition a serious activity, but the current global formulation has overemphasized seriousness, since in the complex global society, virtually everything depends on the functioning of the dragon's system. The trouble is that the present structures are not easily manageable. The change in scale has made the process much more complex. Playing with alternatives has become much more risky. The most recent economic crisis is an example of the unpredictable effects that extended human meaning-making can have. Playful bankers experimented with new products, the consequences of which were not clear beforehand. The crisis that emerged has no easy solution. Another example of the vulnerability of the system can be seen in 9/11. The campaign against terrorism, including the Iraq and Afghanistan wars, can be viewed as a desperate effort to regain control.

Yet the common self-image of the modern human being is optimistic. He or she believes in future solutions for current problems, and even ignores setbacks. Progress is considered natural, not cultural. The blessings that modernization brought are easily extrapolated into the future, projecting visions of an ever better society. And in fact, although there is still no cure for the common cold, many diseases can be treated, especially those that for centuries seemed lethal. The taming of cancer and AIDS is the next chapter in medical history. One need not appeal to works of science fiction to have faith in real science's constant innovation.

Not only medical science, but science in general, provides the clearest example of virtually uncontrolled signification. Whereas the founding fathers of the sciences set the course, with subsequent flows of groundbreaking innovation (see the Nobel prizes), today's academic research moves on the micro-level of the micro-level. I myself serve as an example of this, given that I wrote my PhD thesis on boys' initiation rituals within a tiny tribe of fishermen in Congo. I spent four years of my life studying, analyzing, and describing that ritual.[7] It did not end there. I am still writing about the role of play that I first uncovered in that ritual. Yet, this book is an effort to make up for the long time spent fumbling around and bring my results to the macro level.

The most recent additions to the abundance of existing meaning-making is widespread. Consumerism is part of the dragon's system. Whereas in pre-modern times only the elite, monarchs, and nobles could consume without limit, in late modern times consumable goods are available to a significant and diverse cross-section of humanity. Ironically consumables are frequently less available to those who produce these goods, since it is low incomes that make cheap mass production possible. The number of goods on the market is endless. For every single product, such as a car or PC, there are many types and brands. Although different, they all serve the same purpose and are interchangeable. Here again exaggerated meaning-making has struck hard.

The situation is paradoxical. On the one hand, there are improvements in the quality of human life, thanks to increasing wealth and sophisticated medical care, as exemplified by a significant increase in the average human life span. On the other hand, overpopulation is a problem, given the impossibility of satisfying the basic need for food, and given the patchiness of access to improved medical realities. The paradoxes are not limited to the fields of wealth and health. In fact, modernization brings both progress and setbacks. The modern human meaning-maker is the sorcerer's apprentice. Although human history shows that perfection was always just beyond our reach, the current unprecedented scale and complication keeps us far from the ideal, whatever the ideological imprint of that ideal. The four main global problems mentioned in the Introduction—poverty, violence, pollution, and conflict—reveal the double character of human achievements since modernization. The playful sorcerer's apprentice ventured out into the precarious show he started and now has to run it. His master is nowhere to be seen to repair the damage. So human playfulness in meaning-making is not just a success story. The game has gotten out of hand.

The large human brain is a human asset, but a setback as well. It is not simply a matter of evolution, but of devolution as well. Control over the

7. Droogers, *Dangerous Journey*.

capacity for human meaning-making is problematic. Neoteny was a setback from the start, but meaning-making, the tool that should compensate neoteny, conflated several unfortunate uncontrollable variables. The variety of human ways of life causes conflicts that are difficult to control. A strong sense of identity forges people together, as a means of bonding, but it also separates them from others. Where resources are scarce, as is frequently the case, as economists teach us, competition between groups is ignited. The latest issue of this kind results in the question: who owns the North Pole?

An especially problematic aspect of our times is the capacity for great evil, thought out in the detail, such as the Nazi, Khmer Rouge, and Rwanda killing machines. Earlier human history contains other examples and there is no end to the existence of killing fields. Humans are able to perceive fellow humans in the way that they would another species, as sub-human beasts. This awakens the hunter-predator in humans.

The Domesticated Animal

Although the human being pictures himself as the king of the animal kingdom, he is in fact a handicapped animal that must be pitied. The supposed blessing of human brainpower is a curse in disguise. As we will see in chapter five, the human animal is not even able to keep a sound balance between the hemispheres of his brain. The human being exhibits himself as the director of the zoo, but lives in a cage as well. Humans are the only animals to wear clothes, but their only universal garment is a straightjacket. They are conditioned by an overdose of reflection, addicted to discovering new horizons endlessly. They have become a rudderless missile. Modernization, commonly pictured as progress, has magnified the problematic side of human signification and made it more visible than ever. The human being is a failed experiment in evolution. The playful human being is not built for fun alone. That is the lesson of the last two centuries.

Interestingly, from the very start, human beings have imposed limits on unrestricted playful meaning-making, as if the consequences were already visible to all. There are control mechanisms built into human social life. Obviously group life is impossible when each individual makes use of their limitless capacity for reflection and experiment. It would be extremely impractical if every alternative was in principle always viable and put to use. Chaos would be the inevitable result. Existing cultures and societies are the result of curbing the endless possibilities for human meaning-making.

The widespread diversity among the human species' way of life stems from the need to restrain wild meaning-making.[8] In human beings, the cultural and the social serve as inevitable inbuilt safety valves. The herd domesticates the meaning-making human animal. Human signification is contained by reducing its outcome to limited and relatively fixed ways of meaning-making, preferably with some continuity from one generation to the other. The precise form of cultures and societies puts an end to the flourishing of a thousand flowers. A nice small bouquet is cut from the multitude of possibilities, each society and culture composing its own bouquet from among the many flowers available, and labeling it as normal—lilies for the French, tulips for the Dutch, chrysanthemums for the Japanese. From time to time the bouquet is refreshed, but it will always be a selection. Human repertoires reduce the number of options available. To give an anthropological example, in organizing kinship, one society might follow the fathers' line, another the mothers', and a third society may combine both in some way. In agriculture, some societies focus on cattle, some on grain, others on both. In politics, some societies opt for a strong leader, others for a federative model, while some alternate between models. In all cases, human beings are socialized by their culture and society, to make reduced use of the meaning-making capacity, introducing a light version. This makes life efficient and predictable, while allowing for change. Domesticated and yet potential meaning-making is everywhere. In day-to-day practice people move between the pole of the unlimited thinkable and the pole of the normal—seemingly permanent—scope. At all times the alternatives are kept in reserve and in check.

Power is an important tool in taming human meaning-making capacity. As we saw already, it is the capacity, as human as meaning-making and play itself, to influence other people's behavior, even against their will. The role of influence is significant, because it shows how people are obliged to do what they would not be ready to do of their own volition. Power controls their imagination. It puts a check on their meaning-making play. Play and power are subservient to each other, as in an unhappy marriage, not dissolvable even by mutual consent. The fluid and the solid come as an eternal pair.

8. To me this is not synonymous to the "savage mind" ("*la pensée sauvage*") that Claude Lévi-Strauss discussed, which he viewed as rational and in a particular way scientific. Lévi-Strauss, *La pensée sauvage*.

Interestingly, the emancipation of the authentic individual in the late modern era has created a new situation. Power is still imposed, but the individual has attained much more room for choice, even though the social framework is never far away. Individualization has maintained social dimensions, despite the staring role of the individual.[9] To be authentic is society's command. And yet, individualization has spurred on freedom, as exemplified by democracy and free enterprise. At the same time, new technologies and the increase in the scale of the global have brought forth new forms for the exercise of power. In the development of arms, this has led to the production of high tech precision missiles. Nuclear devices have been developed that are potentially able to destroy the earth. Without even being launched they reach their target, because politicians use them to threaten and deter each other, changing geo-political relations in the process. Industries producing consumer goods have used individual authenticity to market diversity, yet limiting variety to allow for mass production. With just a few hundred shoe-styles, Nike is able to attend to a global clientele. The application of technology has resulted in different means of communication, reaching many people within seconds, as shown by the CNN "Breaking News" items. The mass media effectively influences people's views. The late modern playful animal has ample opportunity to play, but is paradoxically curtailed in her or his meaning-making.

Religious Difference and Similarity

Once human meaning-making is domesticated, how much room is left for imagination, change, and variety? And how does this affect religion? Is there similarity behind diversity?

Let us look once more at the women in the fishermen's village. They play with alternatives when they imagine Esteban's former life, even though they cannot be sure what his real life was like, just as they cannot know what his real name was. And yet they accept the reality of their play, taking what they imagine seriously. They act as though they have been imbued with an overdose of the capacity for reflection. They reify their vigil dreams to daylight reality. They show that they are perfectly able to make sense of the abnormal drowned man and therefore of the vicissitudes of their day-to-day lives. The result is a transformed worldview. Playfulness was

9. Houtman et al., *Paradoxes of Individualization*. See also Elliott and Lemert, *The New Individualism*.

temporarily set free of its usual safehouse. However, as we will see in chapter four, playfulness will be constrained again.

Though fictional, the example offers an image of what happens repeatedly in many religious contexts, with different catalysts, but in similar ways. With this powerful account, Márquez offers a keen insight into religious matters and human meaning-making. Religion, viewed as a universal human capacity, focuses on an extra dimension of reality, manifesting itself in a great variety of forms. Concrete religions, though sometimes similar, use the universal ability of unlimited meaning-making in very different ways. As we saw, all religions may proffer perspectives on basic questions such as what is good, for example, or about life and death, just as they each have rituals relating to specific occasions, such as transitions in life. However, the concrete form and content differ greatly.

In fact, the variation is greater than can be expressed in any textbook on religion and religions. Usually the focus in such introductions is on the five world religions and their differences, but there are thousands of tribal religions as well, each with its own views and practices. Besides, each world religion harbors a number of modalities and factions that compete with each other. Diversity always occurs between generations, even in conservative groups when the young say that they wish to be faithful to the views and practices of their elders. The diversity in meaning-making is even made stronger, because in any religion individual signification produces idiosyncratic results.

Moreover, in the course of time, new religions emerge. Although modernization, as the application of science and technology in society, seems to promote the secular perspective by going against religious worldviews, the reaction to modernization has also been a wave of new religious movements, from Pentecostalism and African Independent Churches, via Cargo Cults, to New Age groups. New opportunities for increased communication have created the opportunity for combining ideas and practices from different religious sources, leading to syncretistic forms. Proselytism has occurred on an unprecedented scale, especially within Christianity and Islam, resulting not only in the conversion of new believers, but also in new mixtures of belief. Converts speak the new religion with the accent of the former worldview. Inevitably they are loyal to both the old and the new, even when saying they abhor the old. The endless possibilities that come with playful human meaning-making are therefore clearly observable in the field of religions.

As I suggested with regard to culture and society, any religion can be said to serve as a way of managing the unlimited possibilities that are available to the human meaning-maker. The water from the universal source of inexhaustible meanings is nicely channeled into the navigable landscape of mainstream religions. Bordering is part of this process. As a cultural phenomenon, within a particular society, and with the influence exerted by its own power mechanisms, religion is part of the effort to curb excessive signification. Any exclusive religious tradition—that is, most religions—contributes to this taming down of the monstrous human possibilities for meaning-making. Paradoxically, diversity is the consequence of the taming of boundless meaning-making. If one were to list, one by one, all the separate ingredients that can be found in the world's religions, the inventory of what human beings can come up with in terms of unlimited playful meaning-making would remain limitless. Even the common elements that are studied in the phenomenology of religion,[10] such as ritual, myth, divinity, sacrifice, prayer, mysticism, Scripture, etc., could not represent the bounds of religious meaning-making, despite the effort to look beyond what separates for what unites. Symbols can be used (for example, the path or way, the wheel, water, fire, etc.), but the meanings given to these symbols are sufficiently diverse to make for very idiosyncratic identities. Yet within their own context, religions impose a clear sense of what must be considered normal, excluding possibilities that in other religions may represent the perfect norm. One religion's gods thus may become another religion's devils. For example, Brazilian Pentecostals condemn the gods and spirits that are central to Afro-Brazilian religions. Even factions within one religion may condemn each other, as when Muslim Salafists destroy the sanctuaries of their Sufi fellow believers, as happened recently.

And yet, amid all this diversity a common basis can be found. As was suggested in chapter one, all religious diversity has its roots in symbolic activity, which provides the constant factor. Symbolizing allows for communication and understanding between believers, even of different religions. Believers are able to recognize the playful meaning-maker in each other. Although different symbolic repertoires may be in use in different settings, they are employed in similar ways, appropriate to the use that the human animal makes of symbols. In chapter five we will see how this shared ability has its physical basis in the structure of the human brain.

---

10. For a recent overview, see Cox, *Introduction to Phenomenology of Religion*.

Let us recall some of the characteristics of symbols. Symbols extend beyond themselves and bring order where it is lacking. They often come connected in a systematic manner, such as in sets of oppositions, allowing for a play with contrasts and inversions. Interestingly, and despite the striking diversity, the number of sources that provide elements that are able to be used as religious symbols is limited. As we saw already, Márquez's fishermen's village is certainly not unique in using the margin and the body as sources. Symbols serve to limit the overcapacity in human meaning-making, acting as instruments for sensible use. Human meaning-making will only happen effectively when kept in check. The stress or insanity that endless possibilities would unleash, is remedied by the properties of the symbol itself. Free meaning-making has its limits. Paradoxically, the problem is at the same time the solution. The limiting tool is supplied along with the abundance.

But there is more to be said on this. As we saw, symbols can stand for what is abstract, invisible, absent, and future-oriented. Thus, to give profane examples of each of these four references, the Stars and Stripes represent abstract nationalism, the iCloud symbol stands for a sector of the invisible Web, the dollar bill represents the imaginary gold kept in the bank, and the sunset refers to the last stage of a person's life. In religions, the abstract, invisible, absent, and future are essential components, each corresponding to characteristics that can be attributed to the sacred. Since symbols are subservient to the intention to express something that is not the symbol in itself, symbols are most helpful in pointing to another, non-human, sacred reality. Through the use of symbols, play with two ways of classifying reality is waged. The women around Esteban's corpse applied this human gift for the use of symbols when they imagined what Esteban stands for: happiness, success, love, the erotic, and even the secret word that makes a woman pick a flower and put it in her hair.

Again, what is common is simultaneously a source of diversity. Depending on the concept of God, gods, spirits, or impersonal forces, symbols express the four salient characteristics—abstract, invisible, absent, and future-oriented—to differing degrees. Believers symbolically extend the parameters of their reality, becoming concerned with and relating to a reality that is at once abstract, invisible, absent, or future-oriented, and that therefore escapes empirical verification. Since symbols extend beyond themselves, the use of symbols, and the unique human capacity to work with them, can be identified as the main tool of religion, going beyond the concrete, the visible and the present in space and in time, adding a new dimension. This human gift by definition manifests itself in diversity. Such a perspective on religion can by way of comparison be contrasted with a perspective on science, as a different field of human meaning-making. Science is concerned with the concrete, the visible, with what is present in space and time, and with that which is open to empirical observation. Knowledge produced via religions, by contrast, expressly moves beyond the observable. Modernization, as the application of science and technology, has reinforced the contrast between religious and empirical knowledge, suggesting the existence of an opposition between failed and true knowledge. The question remains as to whether this distinction holds when viewed from a playful perspective. In chapter six, I return to this issue when reconsidering the God Debate.

Conclusion

Human nature had to be explored before religion could be explained. The long digression contained here was necessary in order for me to be able to move toward a discussion of a theory of religion. Contrary to the typical crowning glory-of-creation rendering, I presented the human animal as a product of devolution, an addict overdosed on reflective capacity. Particularly the modern version of this peculiar animal is problematic. So-called progress has complicated the trouble, regression being a much more apt characterization. Playful meaning-making is not without risks. To be able to function, the human animal must be domesticated. Religion offers one way to achieve this. Yet, as I will show, the risk is that play is eliminated. What can be learned about bordering religions in particular on the basis of this?

When I Have Fears

When I have fears that I may cease to be
Before my pen has gleaned my teeming brain,
Before high-piled books, in charactery,
Hold like rich garners the full ripened grain;
When I behold, upon the night's starred face,
Huge cloudy symbols of a high romance,
And think that I may never live to trace
Their shadows with the magic hand of chance;
And when I feel, fair creature of an hour,
That I shall never look upon thee more,
Never have relish in the faery power
Of unreflecting love; – then on the shore
Of the wide world I stand alone, and think
Till love and fame to nothingness do sink.

—*John Keats*

three

Explaining Religion

Step by Step

NOW THAT THE PORTRAIT of the human animal has been presented, I must take one more preliminary step before I can elucidate my theory of religion. Before setting out such a general view on religion, it is necessary to be aware of the criteria that determine good practice in theorizing religion. This approach offers a way of looking out for the pitfalls, of seeking advance warning. In making this inventory I also seek to gain a better understanding of the interconnections between views on religion from both the outside and the inside. The main issue here is the contrast between science and religion. Theorizing religion, as a scientific task, puts science in the double role of critic and observer. Inevitably the contrast between science and religion—a core issue in this book—often colors theoretical insights on religion. Armed with knowledge about the preconditions for theorizing, I will then examine religion's sources. I will distinguish the central source of excessive reflection from a number of secondary sources, all pointing to the experience of larger wholes that are held in awe. This perspective on religion will then be assessed according to the criteria that I will include in the first section of this chapter. In a final part, the link with the playful approach and with bordering processes will be explored.

Criteria for Theorizing Religion

What are the postulations that govern theorizing religion? Within this framework I will have to situate my contribution to the more general debate on the nature of religion. While offering my own explanation of religion, I will have to keep these methodological considerations in mind.

A first postulation concerns the definition of the concept of religion. To try to define religion is to move through a field of pitfalls. To start with, there is the chicken-and-egg question in any defining task. Anyone who wishes to define religion will start with some prior knowledge—implicit or explicit—of that field, even if only some thoughts on what religion is and what can be considered part of it. This serves as seed money when one starts theorizing. Usually the intuitive notion of what religion is, contains implicit theoretical ideas. Only in the course of the process of defining terms does intuition step aside, ceding the territory to sound theory, which establishes the field with authority and seemingly from scratch. Nevertheless, there is a problem of circular reasoning, with the person doing the defining moving backward and forward, commuting between the poles of induction and deduction. New insights are tested and subsequently adopted or rejected. Consensus and departure are part of the ongoing process.

The results of the defining work undertaken by a range of influential authors, shows the variation of definition types. A common distinction is that between substantial and functional definitions of religion. The substantial approach refers to a presupposed supernatural level about which religious people have some idea. The functional approach defines religion in view of its functions, such as producing knowledge about existential questions, or being a coping mechanism in the midst of afflictions, or serving as the opium of the masses. The functional approach stems from the explanatory framework, making religion intelligible by referring to its functions (e.g., religion as the set of ideas and practices that offer answers to the ultimate questions in life). The substantial approach is primarily descriptive, emphasizing what religion is, more than what it does, for example, religion is defined as a belief in spiritual beings. Usually a substantial definition includes a reference to the sacred, the divine, the holy, or the transcendental. This emphasis may be absent from a functional definition. As a consequence, the functional definition may apply to phenomena that would not fit into the substantial definition, simply because the reference to the sacred is missing. A functional definition could even include other worldviews, such as ideology or nationalism. This means that care must be taken when reading any definition of religion. Is it substantial or functional, or both?

Since religion is uniquely human, a further postulation is that any theory must link religion to exclusively human characteristics. It must therefore seek out universal characteristics, beyond obvious differences. Yet, a theory of religion should not only acknowledge similarity but also diversity. And indeed, efforts have been made to look at religion from this double perspective.[1] These theories are part of the canon of scholars' meaning-making about religion. By way of overview, Stausberg lists four interrelated questions that theories of religion seek to answer.[2] These questions relate to the specificity, the origin, the function, and the structure of religion and religions. Theories of religion address one, some, or all of these questions, showing both similarity and difference in the religious field. The theory of religion that I will present in the next section seeks to include all four questions, showing their connection with what I depicted in the previous chapter as uniquely and universally human, while leaving room for diversity.

As can be expected from what I said about functional definitions, many theories of religion focus on the function of religion, seeking to explain religion's existence from the function it serves: bringing people together, coping with life's difficulties, providing a sense of identity, and several other uses. These functions correspond to general human needs, such as the need for a stable social environment, security, continuity, and predictability. The functional type of theory does not always include a reference to the question of specificity that Stausberg included in his list of four, since all religions are thought to serve these functions, unless it is shown that different religions have different functions. But usually the differences between religions are not addressed within functionalist explanations.

Moreover, religious symbolism contains much more, in terms of narrative and ritual, than is needed in practical terms to reach the result that the functions demand. Any function could well be served by a simple symbolic system, in an almost technical way. Yet, symbolism offers much more than would functionally be needed. Myths and rituals reflect the limitless symbolic imagination, providing more than what would be necessary to bring the group together, to cope with life's afflictions, to provide a feeling of identity, etc. The huge diversity shows that there need not be a direct link

---

1. Clarke and Byrne, *Religion Defined and Explained*; Cunningham, *Religion and Magic*; Jensen and Rothstein, *Secular Theories on Religion*; Pals, *Eight Theories of Religion*; Stausberg, *Contemporary Theories of Religion*; Thrower, *Religion: Classical Theories*.

2. Stausberg, *Contemporary Theories of Religion*, 3–6.

between symbol and function, different symbols having similar functions, similar symbols serving different functions. Functionalist theories ignore symbolic proliferation.

Moreover, the critical question can be raised as to whether a functional theory is sufficiently specific in instances where other phenomena serve the same function. We saw already that a functional definition of religion may include secular nationalisms and ideologies. In the case of Marxism it might include even anti-religious scope (religious in the substantial sense), yet having similar functions. The functions attributed to religion can also be served by other institutions, for example, in the case of the social functions, by kinship or social movements. Besides, those religious phenomena that do not have a clear social function, or that are considered anti-social, such as sorcery and schism, are easily overlooked, and thus left out of the functional explanation. Religion can therefore nourish conflict and disturb social cohesion.

Another critique against the functional explanation of religion asks whether something that can be observed in current religious practice can also be said to have played a role when that religion began. Does a founder of a religion consider its function when beginning a religious movement? If an observer who comes along later attributes a function to the movement, can that function be said to have contributed to its emergence? Or should one make a clear distinction between the outsiders' view and the insiders' religious perspective? In other words, the contrast between observers' and participants' points of view must be taken into consideration when inventing a theory of religion. Believers may establish their own theories on the specificity, the origin, the function, and the structure of their religion, and these may be of interest to the researcher-outsider.

In theorizing religion the contrast between insider and outsider points of view can take more outspoken forms. One such distinction is made between transcendentalist and naturalist theories.[3] Authors of transcendentalist theories accept the insiders' idea that a transcendental entity, whether labeled sacred, divine, holy, or whatever, intervenes and thus is at the origin of religion. Authors of naturalist theories reject this view. The contrast between religion and science, believers and atheists, is herewith introduced into the activity of theorizing religion. The contrast is a historical product

---

3. Stausberg, *Contemporary Theories of Religion*, 11, 12; Thrower, *Religion: The Classical Theories*, 3. The distinction is also known as religionist vs. reductionist, see Droogers, "Methodological Ludism."

of modernization, with its emphasis on the scientific worldview. Thrower[4] typifies the transcendentalist approach by mentioning the possible starting-points of revelation, experience, and the need for a philosophy of life (thus pointing to a function of religion!). In his view, naturalistic theories treat religion either as a primitive error, or as a human, psychological or social construct. Scholars who are in some way believers may combine the two types, as Rudolf Otto and William James have, for example.[5]

Ultimately the core difference between transcendentalist and naturalist theories relates to the question of whether the sacred exists. As already suggested, that question is a product of the modernization process. Naturalist theories, in particular, are thought to reduce the religious to the non-religious, thereby explaining it away, to the satisfaction of those with a secular worldview.[6] To proponents of theories that let some transcendental actor, or even an impersonal energy force play a role in the emergence of religion, this is of course unacceptable.

I suggest that an approach from the perspective of play is able to go beyond this divide, at once showing the unmistakable role of non-religious aspects and maintaining the believers' claim to a transcendent reality. After all, play can only be performed in a serious way and must be taken seriously, even when it is identifiable as play. Since play offers the opportunity to deal simultaneously with two or more ways of classifying reality, it becomes possible to go beyond the transcendentalist vs. naturalist divide. It is no longer necessary to opt for only one way of classifying reality, either transcendentalist or naturalist. As a consequence, justice can be done to both the transcendentalist and naturalist points of view and their particular variants. Thus the believers' way of playing with a transcendental classification of reality can and must be taken seriously, as they themselves take it, though often over-seriously. On the other hand, the naturalist theorist plays in a serious way with meanings, making an effort to connect religious reality with non-religious and academic categories, focusing on specificity, origins, functions, or structures, for example, or looking for some human, social or psychological construct. The scholar may also do so in an overly-serious manner. It is the over-serious attitude of both believer and scholar that reinforces the contrast, whereas the playful approach, even when taken seriously, as it should be, redefines the issue, bridging opposites.

4. Thrower, *Religion: The Classical Theories*.

5. James, *Varieties of Religious Experience*; Otto, *Idea of the Holy*.

6. Stausberg, *Contemporary Theories of Religion*, 286.

Stausberg[7] raises another methodological issue that requires our attention. Over the last decades, the act of theorizing has met with strong criticism from constructivists and postmodernists,[8] who seek to expose the relativistic nature of seemingly true knowledge claims and who remain skeptical of theory and its concepts. The net result has been that scholars have had the opportunity to become more conscious of their purportedly objective, but often subjective, way of dealing with theoretical insights, and that subsequently they take less exclusive positions. I think that the consequence of this should be that religion can be defined not only by its focus on believers, but could also include those who study these believers. In a kaleidoscopic way, academic meaning-makers give meaning to religious meaning-makers, and both seek to give meaning as human animals. Scholars are the people who to a large extent have invented this field of study, developing theories and introducing concepts, refurbishing the category "religion" into the forms we now know. Their role is as much part of the field of study as the role of the believers that they research. In fact, constructivism suggests that academic knowledge is the result of the interaction between researcher and researched.[9] Theory is thereby a self-reflective activity. As I will show in chapter six, this is in keeping with the playful approach and what I call "methodological ludism," since it invites scholars to identify, if only for a short while, with the believers that they study, playing their meaning-making game in as serious a manner, and yet being conscious of the game.

The postmodern point of view demands awareness of the way in which believers and scholars each deal with ways to classify reality, whether religious or scientific, or even both. Much depends on the starting-point one chooses to classify religious reality. Stausberg's edited volume[10] maps many of the scholarly starting-points available, showing the complementarity of points of view that are often employed in an exclusive way.

Taking an eclectic position,[11] I see my own perspective on religion as one among other relevant contributions. My approach is more inclusive

7. Ibid., 12–14.

8. Docherty, *Postmodernism*; Guba, *Paradigm Dialog*; Rosenau, *Post-modernism and the Social Sciences*. On postmodernism and religion, see Berry and Wernick, *Shadow of Spirit*.

9. Guba, *Paradigm Dialog*, 27.

10. Stausberg, *Contemporary Theories of Religion*.

11. Droogers, "From Waste-making to Recycling."

than exclusive. The presupposed play perspective indeed points to the simultaneity of views. It shows theorists playing with different elements and coming to different conclusions. One may have preferences, as I do, but on principle we are all artists making a painting of the same sacred mountain, only from different perspectives and with different means. Some are more interested in specifics, others in origins, or functions, or structures. Some emphasize ontological questions, others start from ethical, epistemological, aesthetic, or identity questions. To some, reason is the starting-point, whereas others look for beginnings in emotional or social experience, or in a need for understanding or salvation.[12] Some see myth as the origin of religion,[13] others ritual,[14] others still, both. Interdisciplinary theorists, looking for explanations, turn to other fields of study, such as linguistics, evolutionary biology, or cybernetics. More recently several theorists have been inspired by cognitive neuroscience.[15] All theorists, myself included, belong to the human animal species of ceaseless, overactive meaning-makers.

All are inspired and yet constrained, we all come with valuable and nevertheless partial insights. At the current stage of detailed scientific meaning-making, which includes the study of religion, no author is able to claim to have a fully elaborated view, even though the perfect theory remains the Archimedean point of reference from which everything can be understood. Nevertheless, here too the selective, light version of human meaning-making is inevitable. Each theory is a limited edition. My approach is no exception.

Having set out these methodological underpinnings, justifying this lengthy discussion in terms of their relevance, we are now ready to look at religion in an effort to utilize these criteria. In formulating an explanation of religion, I present a theory that takes religion to be uniquely human, yet as diverse as human cultures and languages. I will refer to the specificity, origin, function, and structure of religion, understood as both some form of revelation and as a construct. Thus, I seek to avoid the pitfalls of functionalist explanations. I wish to do justice to both believers' and scholars' viewpoints. In doing so, I am aware of my academic subjectivity. I

12. Cf. Stausberg, *Contemporary Theories of Religion*, 267, referring to Riesebrodt.

13. Rue, *Religion is Not about God*; Seiwert, "Theory of Religion as Myth."

14. Rappaport, *Ritual and Religion*.

15. The majority of the authors discussed in Stausberg, *Contemporary Theories of Religion*, use notions from cognitive studies. See also Whitehouse and Laidlaw, *Religion, Anthropology, and Cognitive Science*; Slyke, *The Cognitive Science of Religion*; Visala, *Naturalism, Theism*. In chapter six I will add a cognitive dimension to my approach.

will avoid a unilateral naturalist or reductionist approach. In designing the theory, I will also ask how, within this framework, bordering religion can be understood.

A Theory of Religion: The Basic Source

Let us explore the value of the following affirmation: religion stems from the human experience with phenomena that suggest a larger whole, beyond human control and approached with awe, but that humans nevertheless seek to hold sway over. There are several of these phenomena, and I will discuss them one by one. In this section I will consider *playful reflection*, being the basic source, leaving the discussion of the other sources—*knowledge, time, space, nature, the body, the self, society, communication, evil, music, and, as a newcomer, consumerism*—to the next section. Some of these sources impose themselves on the human animal in a natural way, others are the result of human activity. Together they may seem an odd lot, but they all suggest that there is an "Other" existing "apart from ourselves,"[16] something—or someone—bigger than humans can imagine or control. They nourish awareness in humans of what exceeds their efforts. All these experiences of wholes that are difficult to grasp enhance each other and include the suggestion of a power that exceeds human dimensions.

This set of experiences is full of potential and yet seems threatening. They all represent a manifestation of what lies beyond, challenging human command and inspiring awe. The first and basic experience, that of playful reflection, serves as the paradigmatic awareness of other experiences. Meaning-making is activated when humans experience these unsatisfactory contexts. They all compel the human animal to use his (or her) oversized reflective power to interpret his extraordinary position in that particular context. Signification serves as the instrument to give names and interpretations to these overpowering wholes. When all is said and done, the power to reflect creates the awareness that humans fall short of absolute power.

Yet reflection does more than detect the failure. It evokes the idea of a power beyond human power. The human animal's overblown capacity to reflect is therefore very basic in the birth of religion, focused on some Other. Religion emerges from emergency. In all the phenomena listed above, the effort to gain pre-eminence fails and thus invites new reflection. People continue to seek ways to throw their weight about, however without

16. McGilchrist, *The Master and His Emissary*, 386.

ever becoming fully master of the situation. Sacred power represents and symbolizes this aspect of the human condition. Obdurate as humans are, even sacred power is thereupon subjected to efforts to control it.

To understand this, let us look at the concrete wholes that I mentioned. Since it is the most basic example, the extraordinary human *capacity to reflect on reality*, as described above, is the first to be considered here. It includes the ability to play with meanings and alternatives, contrasts and inversions. Play, as I define it, is the human capacity to deal simultaneously with two (or more) ways of categorizing reality. Thus alternatives can be considered. Because of the human capacity for playfulness, reflection can become a source of joy and satisfaction, making reality manageable and predictable. However, playful reflection can also seem threatening, since it leaves the possibility of alternative approaches wide open. Play therefore introduces not only pleasant associations with leisure and gaiety, but it can also lead people to feel desperate since it always raises new alternatives. Though diverse in range, various kinds of play also introduce their own limits, of inexpressibility and lack of comprehension. People suffer because of this, even bodily, as is clear from the examples of religious virtuosos who were hesitant, or reluctant, when called on to accept a vocation. Some of these were at great pains to refuse the role of religious innovator.

Under these conditions, religion explores the unspeakable and opens it out for communication. Liability is turned into an asset. The infinite possibilities that playful reflection provides, that enable interpretation of any part of human reality, ultimately point to an Other sphere that escapes reflection and is thereby beyond human control. The Judean and Christian commandment "Thou shalt not make unto thee any graven image" (Exod 20: 4) can be read as suggesting that God is more than any image can express. The existential questions mentioned in the Introduction—"Why do humans live and die?" "What is good behavior?" "What is true?" "What is beautiful?" and ultimately, "Who am I?"—are almost all unsolvable. The aesthetic question is perhaps the least thorny of the set, but as the fate of art under dictatorship shows, the answers even in this domain are not unequivocal. The common disappointment stemming from the absence of an answer to these questions has been lyrically cried out as "I can't get no satisfaction," a phrase that made millions. Religious reflection is—literally—wishful thinking that produces the suggestion of the existence of a power, personal or impersonal, bigger than humans, with all the qualities to compensate for human failure and lack of satisfaction. The idea is born in the real and corporeal experience of the beyond, as a result of the oversized human capacity for reflection. The remedy is as embodied as the problem.

In this way the stumbling block caused by an overdose of endless reflection is converted into a solution. The failing human capacity is reversed into a supra-human Other power that never disappoints, since it is what the believer wishes to be but is unable to become. If the possibilities are unlimited, virtue and need are both acknowledged. A seemingly infertile perspective is subsequently categorized into usable concepts of the sacred Other. The capacity of play allows for an alternative categorization of reality, in this case supernatural. Thus, the power to act is returned to the rehabilitated human actor who had failed the admission exam. She or he is thus empowered, playing the believer's or even a priestly role of serving the sacred supernatural. Thereby the existential feeling of lack of control is overcome in a roundabout way. Sacred power leaves a thick residue.

Experiences of loneliness in the face of what surpasses human command are transformed into an awareness of belonging. The human animal that discovered that he or she stood apart, can once again feel part of a larger whole. The unlimited, seemingly uncontrollable meaning-making activity is given a form that enables communication. Even though contact, almost by definition, often falters, in view of the inbuilt inequality of the sacred and human partners in dialogue, it works sufficiently well to be continued.

Interestingly, silence is the recommended attitude in some religions, from Zen to the Quakers. Believers in meditation wait for the Other to speak or for the ultimate silence to be experienced. Even non-reality can be pursued. The relative value of images, words, and terms is recognized in this way, believers abandoning them or being extremely economical, or cryptic in using them. The solution to overblown reflection is to position oneself at the other extreme. Accordingly, conscious reflection is discouraged. Emptiness is a fitting symbol. The power profile of this type of approach is usually interestingly low, power itself being seen to be problematic, although masters may have a central role as well, often paradoxical, more questioning than affirmative. Among modern adherents of this type of approach, modernization's busy meaning-making and infernal din may have provoked a reaction that seeks illumination and fulfillment in implicit meaning. From Enlightenment people move toward Zenlightenment.

Other Sources

This general affirmation, based on one very basic source, must now be tested in the other cases listed above, starting with *knowledge, time, and space*. What ultimately proves impossible to humans in terms of these three categories suggests the possibility of the ultimate sacred, representing the inversion of human failure in these areas, offering compensation and fulfillment. Whereas other animals are not capable of living beyond the moment or the place they find themselves, human animals are able to do so and to reflect on the consequences of this perspective. This opens new horizons, closed to other animals. In his or her symbolic toolkit, the human animal has several instruments to apply to this situation. Contrasts and inversions lead the way to invoke the extraordinary Other, over and against the ordinary. Among the results is the possibility of the overpowering divine. As a consequence, supernatural actors are, in contrast to the human, depicted as all-knowing. Omniscient gods succeed where human knowledge fails. Similarly, the limits of time, symbolized by the end of a person's bodily existence, calls for the idea of endless, uninterrupted time, existing only within the domain of the gods. The existence of the eternal can be contemplated, including recompense in the afterlife. In a similar manner, the limits in space call forth the idea of omnipresence and endlessness, attributed to sacred entities. The human deficit in knowledge, time, and space is thus compensated, adding to the metaphoric vocabulary. Autonomy can be regained by effective communication with the sacred powers.

Another important experience comes from the confrontation with *nature*. This confrontation can seem overwhelming, because of the many species of plants and animals, the magnitude of forests, deserts, and outer space, the sheer size of the earth with its ever-receding horizon, or the uncontrollable lost energy of volcanoes, tornados, floods, and earthquakes. Nature serves as a repertoire for religious metaphors, including the four elements of earth, water, air, and fire, or the Christian fifteenth-century idea of God who can be read in the Book of Nature. Encountering nature, the human animal feels vulnerable, yet seeks control. Religion may form part of this effort, just as economical and political behavior and—more recently— the natural sciences offer other ways of managing this aspect of human reality. Religions come with personal or impersonal labels, with pantheons of gods that divide the natural spheres between them, or suggest the presence of nature spirits, or an anonymous force in nature that rules human lives. Some religions command respect for nature, others legitimate human dominance over nature. The religious worldviews that emerged have come under criticism when the scientific worldview offered an alternative perspective and a mode of human autonomy. Creation and miracles became doubtful concepts. Yet the religious perspective continues to sustain many people's lives.

A further source of the human animal's amazement at her (or his) situation is in relation to her *body*, in fact part of nature, but the part closest to the human experience. Through the body the animal side of the human being imposes itself with dramatic impact. From the very start of a human life, the body appears to be uncontrollable, birth being a risky passage for mother and child. Other animals encounter the same risks, but only humans reflect and exchange views on them. Although over the last centuries medical science has succeeded in protecting the body against many risks, disease is always lurking around the corner, sooner or later bringing death, the ultimate winner. The body is also the tool for reproducing the human species. As a corporeal function, sexuality is a source of special experiences that extend beyond the limits of one body. The supreme moment escapes human control. It is pleasurable but also ecstatic and overwhelming, possibly threatening and risky. Happiness has the body as a locus. Another characteristic of the body is that it requires sleep, and sleep comes with puzzling and uncontrollable dreams, suggesting other realities, with their own classifications. While dreaming, the human imagination is unchecked and therefore at its wildest. The evoked realities play with people, just as people tend to play with them, interpreting what was dreamt. Some people spend years at supervised weekly sessions to play the dream game. People may have visions revealed in dreams, but also in waking state. Bodies come not only with dreams, but also with altered states of consciousness, such as trance and spirit possession. Clairvoyance, divination, auras, foreseeing the future, and healing power are examples of enigmatic experiences. Religions address all the puzzles that come with the human body. They differ in the interpretations they put forward. Some allow just one life to the human animal, others suggest the possibility of more lives. Some promise a new body and reunion with the beloved deceased, while others deny such a possibility. Some view the body as sinful; others see it as the temple of the divine. Some focus on life before death, others on the afterlife. Some seek to heal bodies, others confer the means to cause illness and affliction. And some combine options, despite the eventual contradiction.

Closely related to the body, is yet another source of unsatisfactory experience. Human animals are able to use their gift for reflection to invent the *self*. The immense outer space finds its parallel in endless inner space. Human animals spend their life reflecting on the question "Who am I?" In this search they may get lost. Religions have suggested a vocabulary for self-understanding, including concepts of spirit and soul, possibly suggesting eternity. They offer maps for life's course and the hereafter. These may include moral ingredients, invested in the responsible self. Science has entered this domain as well, mapping the landscape of the self in psychology, offering "self"-help. With modern individualization, the focus on the self is now of central interest to culture and society. The autonomous authentic self may feel liberated and emancipated, yet, being fragmented, it may also look desperately for certainty and connection, having lost its way. Limitless reflection about one's identity, frightening in itself, becomes even more alarming when conducted in front of the mirror. Where science, especially psychotherapy, fails to help, religions continue to serve as providers of models for the self, saved or condemned, divine or sinful, unified or multiple, harmonious or at war with itself.

The latest version of this process can be seen in the supposed migration of God from out there to the inner self, also described as the spiritual revolution.[17] The meaning-making human animal appears to have completed the circle, returning God from the outward projection to the inner locus of human signification, the reflecting self. The inner God can be a source of empowerment, just as the outward God once was, though in a different way. Self-esteem is reinforced. The personality's whole is reflected in the divine nature of the self. The accompanying concept of God contains the modern self's qualities as well as its problems, including its fragmentation and dualisms. The list of basic existential questions presented in the Introduction still applies here. The inner God may have some of the characteristics of the former outer God, such as being a moral compass, now located in the person's conscience. That inner God may also serve to legitimate some deep insights the person may discover in the self and all by himself (or herself). That God may also sanction a person's identity to be authentic and true. The real pitfall of the divine self is loneliness. The self may wish to stand apart but cannot live without being part. Even the focus on the self is a social find, a cultural commandment. Living in relationship with others demands a common basis, also when the participants see

17. Heelas and Woodhead, *Spiritual Revolution*.

themselves as original and possibly divine selves. In the end, the self and the God within are the constructs of the person who seeks them, results of the play with concepts and meanings, taken seriously, designed for lack of better alternatives. As a source of religion, the self has to find its place next to the other sources. When deception via the outer God opens the way to the God within, people may in the long run experience similar problems with the inner God (e.g., remaining silent, hiding himself). Remarkably, most atheist criticism has so far left the inner God outside the God Debate, as if the main problem with the outer God is his external position in relation to people.

Society is another source for the experience of what outclasses the human animal. Society existed before the person's birth, and will survive long after his death. It has the authority to reward and to punish its members. It imposes rules and moral conscience. It brings people together and guarantees a certain degree of order. It may channel mutual help and diminishes the loneliness of its members. As Durkheim suggested,[18] the social experience nourishes religion. Social gatherings may evoke the sensation of something major that transcends the individual.

Typically the characteristics of society as a whole are, as Durkheim suggested,[19] attributed to divinity as well: rewarding and punishing, imposing moral behavior, legitimating order, acting as a source of help and bringing people together. Society serves as a model for the way the divine is thought about, just as the inverse may happen, sacralizing society and its leaders. As a tool in society's dominance, power easily enters religious vocabulary, social power serving as a metaphor for divine power, divine power legitimating secular power, as I will discuss in the next chapter. Sharing these characteristics, strong power structures with a high degree of institutionalization may correspond with similar concepts of gods and God in that same society. The social and the religious may mirror and reinforce each other. Thus monotheism seems to emerge in a situation where unity is needed, in the social, political and economic fields, bringing with it the risk of inviting exclusive self-serving power.

And then there are human-made forms of wholes that nevertheless escape human control. In fact, society could be viewed as such a form, the

18. Durkheim, *Elementary Forms.*

19. "[R]eligion is eminently social. Religious representations are collective representations which express collective realities. . . . So if the categories are of religious origin, they ought to participate in this nature common to all religious facts; they too should be social affairs and the product of collective thought." Durkheim, *Elementary Forms,* 10.

social understood as a given with the human animal's nature, yet resulting in an immense variety of organizational types for the human herds, contrary to other animals' social behavior. Here are some examples of other human products that evoke the experience of the beyond that resists control.

Thus human *communication* suffers from the tension between success and failure, comprehension and altercation. Symbols help in expressing experiences, but easily create misunderstanding. Metaphors "always contain the whisper, 'it is *and it is not*.'"[20] The unthinkable becomes thinkable, but with ambiguous results. The unbounded range of metaphors, with successive layers of meaning, may drive even the best poet or philosopher crazy, as has been known to happen. The empire of meanings rules and cannot be fully contained.

Modernization has given birth to extreme forms of communication, as is most obvious in the mass media. The best metaphor for modern forms of excessive meaning-making is the number of hits on any topic in Google, delivering information in unmanageable quantities. Modern computer communication now uses the metaphor of the cloud, interestingly a traditional image of divine presence, by definition always located above humans. Even modern communication thus indirectly sustains the basic human experience of the beyond.

All *evil* planned and executed in the course of human history belongs within this human-made category. I remember the shock, when visiting the city of Weimar in Germany, where the heroes of *Zivilisation*, such as Goethe and Schiller had lived and worked, to discover that the Buchenwald concentration camp was located at a mere ten kilometers from the city center. The site, or what is left of it, is depressing, but most disconcerting of all was the complexity of detail contained within the system. The cynical words on the iron main gate to the camp read: "*Jedem das Seine*," "to each his own," originally a Latin phrase "*Suum cuique*." One may blame the Nazis responsible for the invention of this system of destruction. However, evil is certainly not a German prerogative alone, but is a given of the human capacity for unlimited meaning-making. In the moral context as well, meaning-making is without limits, for better or for worse, also in the sense that it is able to make bad guys out of well-intended good guys.[21] Moral rules about good behavior are of course the result of the same meaning-making

20. McFague, *Metaphoric Theology*, 13, italics in original.

21. For a moving and profound account, among many others, see Antelme, *The Human Race*, on his experiences in Nazi extermination camps.

capacity. Religions have thus been part of the promotion of both good and evil, legitimating and also explaining both, in shifting contexts. The beyond that triggers the human imagination includes evil as a possibility. Evil gods have been the result, just as the origins of evil have been explained in a variety of myths. Evildoers may feel they exert control, whereas their victims are subjected to power. Both sides use the human gift for meaning-making and both may include elements from religious repertoires when experiencing the evil beyond.

The four global problems—poverty, violence, pollution, and conflict—not only bear witness to the human shortcomings in purposeful meaning-making, but also contain a moral dimension. Evil takes modern forms, sometimes not recognized as evil, with religious groups acting as stakeholders on both sides. Humanity is scarcely able to manage the complex world society that is its modern product. Here as well the presence of something evil, bigger than man, is felt.

There are other forms of human activity that create the sense of the existence of a beyond, for example *music*. Music is sometimes called divine, a direct religious metaphor. In my de-churching homeland, The Netherlands, the traditional Sunday morning visit to a church service has, for a cohort of music lovers, been substituted with a similar amount of time spent in the so-called coffee concert, at eleven AM or noon. The musical performance may take place in a church building, either still in use, or transformed for artistic purposes. Religious music remains popular. The annual performances of Bach's *Matthew Passion* attract large audiences, including many people who have taken their leave from religion. Other musical events may involve a major gathering of people, such as pop concerts, conveying the sense of something major and indescribable taking place. Marching music can produce the same social effect, as part of nationalism or ideology, with mass meetings or parades acting as expressions of something bigger than the individual and providing a special thrill to those present. Religious elements may be part of that setting.

A contemporary example of the experience of the beyond, based on human artifacts that are part of the capitalist system, can be found in *consumerism*. The immense possibilities that the consumer has at her (or his) disposal, provided she derives adequate income, suggest a dimension of reality that is bigger than the single consumer. The market rules. Dufour[22] suggests that nowadays the major religion of the world is that of the market,

22. Dufour, *Le Divin Marché*, 17.

serving as the paradigm for many human relations. In his view, the market is the substitute for the God that lost the secularization battle, at least in Western European countries. Just as society and divinity share characteristics, the God of the market, as the new "beyond," is the twin brother of the Christian God. Not coincidentally, Adam Smith, one of the first to analyze the emerging market, was a theologian.[23] His belief was that the market will provide, redressing problems, just as the Christian God did.[24] Once again the modernization process, which has significantly altered the face of the earth, has been important in putting this new liberal God, that Dufour calls perverse,[25] on the throne. The dragon rules. The main commandments of the new religion are "Enjoy!"[26] and "Don't worry, be happy!" Consumers celebrate their individuality, but are in fact controlled by the herd.[27] The human ability for play is abused.

Here too, for a group other than the music lovers in my country, there is a substitute for the Sunday morning church service. It involves a ride to the nearest shopping mall, the consumers' new temple. A new word has been added to the Dutch vocabulary: *Koopzondag* ("Buying Sunday"). Whether on Sundays or weekdays, the thrill of buying a new product fulfills the consumer's understanding of happiness, satisfaction now on sale. The mere act of making a purchase may be sufficient, the subsequent use of the goods purchased may not be necessary to sustain the kick. Marketing toys with metaphors that previously were the domain of religion: "Discover the divine magic of perfume X!"

Speaking of experiencing the beyond through humanity's own projects, *religion* itself could be added to the list. The various sources of the religious dimension discussed so far are neutral and profane. They are not usually considered as religious, although references to religious symbolism may occur in day-to-day language regarding these sources, just as they may provide metaphors that express the religious concern with the divine. Nature and society have always served as sources of religious metaphors. But once religion exists, it may, like the other sources mentioned, obtain characteristics that escape human control, thereby confirming and reinforcing the effect of the other sources. The God or gods thus refer to the

23. Ibid., 102.
24. Ibid., 132.
25. Ibid., 17.
26. Ibid.
27. Ibid., 26.

other sources, serving as a summation of them all. The sources are reflected in a religions' metaphoric repertoires.

Especially when a religion succeeds in providing answers to the basic existential questions listed in the Introduction, its authority is established, turning religion into an additional source, in a self-confirming autocratic way. In the quest for satisfactory solutions to ontological, ethical, episte-mological, aesthetic, and identity questions, the various sources are used in a most effective and helpful way. Maximum use is made of the fact that they are located outside and above the believer, furnishing the elements that humans do not have at their disposal. All questions can receive plau-sible answers, because the sources are not only functional, but moreover address issues of content, serving as repertoires of metaphors, thus making religious diversity possible. The variety of sources is thereby reflected in the diversity of the answers given, within and outside a particular religion. Each religion can be viewed as representing a heteronym of the divine, just as the Portuguese poet Fernando Pessoa used heteronyms to write very diverse poems.

The role of religion itself as a source is illustrated in the Christian case, in which the church institution is viewed as a holy, supra-individual gathering place, having its own dynamics, over and above the faithful, who as subjects are subjected to it, and eventually turned into objects. The in-stitution appears as if it were a giant actor on its own, stronger than the believer and surviving him or her through the ages. Muslims may express similar sentiments regarding the umma. In addition, in the organization of any religious institution, rituals and convictions may become so complex that only specialists are able to understand the intricacies contained within them. As if spread via a process of contamination, the sacred nature of the divinity passes on to the institution. Veneration for the institution is then a source of belief in the transcendental, just as complex rituals may be, like the visualization of the institution, including the domain reserved for spe-cialized priests in its leadership. The class of religious specialists may serve as another whole, the frock being positioned above the flock. The clergy can be perceived by the average believer as belonging to a higher order, as if its members participate in the divine.

Christian theology can be viewed as the charter of the church as insti-tution. It is a complex constellation of continuous meaning-making about the five existential questions, working with the accumulated answers of twenty centuries. Its status is so high that what to the outsider would seem a minor change, is presented as a giant step. The result is an immense corpus of dogma and exegesis, the secrets of which are only available to very specialized scholars. The importance of the church institution is reflected in the existence of ecclesiology as a special theological sub-discipline. The laity are often uninformed.

After this inventory of the wholes that serve as religion's sources, and in view of the prominent role they play in my explanation of religion, one may ask whether in existing religions these wholes can be shown to actually receive attention. In my view a typology can be developed, showing the diversity of options available with regard to wholes and identifying the choices that are made. Even within one religion, factions may exist, differing in their answers and even in their options, despite the common roots. The distinction between official and popular religion also suggests different positions within one religion, closely related to the power distribution.

When comparing religions, one basic choice when selecting a particular view, is between a dualistic way of thinking and the possibility of a monistic perspective, the latter solving the tension that is inherent within the dualistic position. Taking this option as the starting-point, a variety of attitudes towards the whole can be distinguished. Thus the sacred can be depicted as a whole that is different from human reality, but is also an integral part of reality, perhaps its grounding essence. Another question is whether the sacred is viewed as personal, or as an anonymous force, or even as the totality of what exists. If taken to be a personal force, the options include polytheist and monotheist positions, but may also contain the idea of the continued presence of ancestor spirits in the society of the living, as if they were still around, available for consultation. One particular option gives a place to nature spirits, nature being one of the wholes that were listed as sources. The human reality may also be experienced as one in which everyone is thought to be connected with everyone, the community of believers forming the ideal society. This is another way of giving the idea of a whole a place in a worldview, with the theocratic model as the most outspoken form, possibly accompanied by the justification of self-serving power. Another question that is answered in religions is whether the whole of time and space includes life beyond death, with the follow-up question regarding whether humans have more lives to live, or just one. The whole may be thought to encompass a long series of lives. Reincarnation in Eastern religions can be contrasted with the Christian idea of resurrection. The whole may also inspire the idea that the universe is one, coupled with the advice: be one with the universe! Such an approach may play with the paradox of fullness and emptiness. As we saw, silence can be a variation on the theme of emptiness, the most radical reaction to the tumultuous meaning-making that is the human animal's tragic ability, especially under modern circumstances.

Admittedly, this way of mapping the religions of the world is rather rough and the typology is very tentative. Each religion has its own way of dealing with the sources that were identified as feeding the religious experience. This also makes the variety in repertoires complex. The list of the wholes that serve as sources can therefore in itself be the starting-point of a typology, taking their metaphoric use into account.

In summarizing what has been said so far in seeking to explain religion, a definition of religion was implicit, and sometimes its elements were explicit. Although, as we saw, many definitions have been proposed already,[28] the approach suggested here would endorse the following definition: *religion is the set of ideas and practices, referring to a superhuman reality, that humans develop in compensation for their unsatisfactory experiences with both excessive reflection and larger wholes, enabling them to regain a sense of control over a reality that escapes their command.* This definition has a clear functional component, pointing to the element of compensation. Yet it also contains a substantial element, since it presents the reality with which humans seek to be connected beyond human control, thereby pointing to all those characteristics that turn human failure into sacred dominance.

A Sound Theory?

Before formulating this explanation of religion, I mentioned a few conditions that must be dealt with in the search for plausible theory. Did I mention what is uniquely human in the playful approach? Does my version convey something about the origin, structure, specificity, and function of religion, as some form of revelation or construct? Were the functionalist pitfalls avoided? Have I given a place to both believers' and scholars' viewpoints? Am I aware of possible subjectivity in my explanation? Did I succeed in avoiding reductionism?

The uniquely human characteristic of overblown playful reflection was interpreted as the basic source of the religious experience. Its paradoxical combination of unlimited potential and uncontrollable capacity is

28. Droogers, "Defining Religion," 263–79.

a universal human condition. I suggested that religion inverts the setback into an asset, clothing the sacred with the characteristics that humans fail to realize. Subsequently the sacred is available to compensate for human shortcomings. Believers feel empowered. Seeking an explanation of religion in the human condition is a way of determining its origin.

Does this theory contribute to an understanding of religion's structure? The fact that the sacred is supposed to possess the capacities that humans lack, implies a vertical relationship, characterized by dependency. The weak party in the bond, the believers, seek to regain control. Feeling overwhelmed, they wish to be empowered, tapping into sacred energy. This structural starting-point colors the ideas and practices that are subsequently developed. It corresponds nicely with dual power structures in profane society, which serve as a repertoire of metaphors.

The aspect of revelation is integrated into this theory by taking the playful human attitude with regard to wholes as a presupposition, admitting the idea of communication with this Other and thus with revelation. Since play is a serious activity, this categorization of reality that is the outcome of playful meaning-making must be taken seriously. That is what believers do, even in an exaggerated measure, as a consequence of the serious nature of existential questions. Since power plays a significant codifying and organizing role from the start, play is gradually replaced with seriousness. Revelation is an expression of this seriousness. As a consequence, a tentative interpretation of the visionary founder's experience with the beyond is reified into a timeless and institutionalized truth. In this way the theory honors the believers' point of view, and not just the scholars'. The playful explanation of religion is not fully reductionist, although secular aspects form part of the approach. I will return to this theme when I discuss playful religion in chapter five. There too, the view of religion as a construct, another item in the list of criteria for a theory of religion, will receive attention.

What does this approach to understanding religion tell us about the specificity of religion? I sought to interrogate religion's special role in conveying supra-human characteristics attributed to the sacred, and in its corresponding function to complement the incomplete human apparel. In serving this goal, religion not only confers compensation for the human impossibility of managing the overdose of reflection, but at the same time it redresses the inconvenience caused by the hampering of the signification process, thereby empowering its believers. The transformation of the uncanny whole into an Other that can be approached and addressed, is religion's contribution to the human animal's struggle with his contradictory outfit.

Consequently, the criterion that insists that a theory of religion should include its function has been met. I attribute to religion the role of complementing, rectifying the unmanageable human capacity for meaning-making. But did I avoid the functionalist pitfall? This criterion needs a more detailed treatment.

The critique against functionalist explanations of religion is, as we saw, that secular ideologies and other sectors of society may have similar functions, thereby leaving the unique specificity of religion outside the explanation. A criticism has therefore been that the religious is reduced to the secular. It was also argued that religion may work in ways contrary to these functions, for example, by being anti-social. These explanations reason backwards, from the consequence to the cause, as if the religion's founder intended to serve a particular function.

The specific nature of religion, connected with the belief in a sacred entity, is a direct result of the idea that the sacred Other is capable of doing what humans are unable to do. Divine behavior is anthropomorphically defined by reference to human capacities, yet without their shortcomings. Although this implies the function of compensation, it is directly connected with the specific nature of the sacred. It not only shows what the sacred *does*, that is, in functional terms, but also what the sacred *is*, in terms of symbolic substantial content. The playful explanation includes the rich symbolism of religions, which is the direct result of the human capacity for ample meaning-making. The possibility to consider religion in terms of revelation that the playful approach offers, underpins the specificity of religion. Even the anti-social function of religion finds a place in the playful explanation, as was evident from the discussion of evil as one of religion's sources. In conclusion, the functionalist pitfall was avoided, without omitting reference to the function that religion has. In chapter five, I will return to the functionalist explanation.

Finally, I must note my awareness of the possibility that my explanation is subjective. The answer could be a short "yes, of course," but it could also lead to an autobiographical digression. Fortunately such an account already exists and is available in the public domain. The Introduction to my collected essays, published under the title *Play and Power in Religion*,[29] is an autobiographical essay explaining my path through the discipline and the

---

29. Droogers, *Play and Power in Religion*.

field, showing how I developed my views. What I said about my grandson Sam also highlights my subjective approach.

The Playful Perspective on Bordering Religion

In explaining religion in this manner, what did we learn about bordering religions? What is the value of the playful approach for our understanding of bordering processes? Is there any link between the over-reflective human animal, seeking to live with the experience of wholes that are beyond her or his control, and the bordering tendency in these religions? The beginning of an answer can be given here, yet, the discussion can only be completed in the next chapter, when I add power to the mix.

It is precisely their bordered nature that appears to make bordering religions apt at playing the redressing role *in optima forma*. They represent the most striking examples of what has been defined above as an explanation of religion. The compensation that religion offers, both in terms of overactive human meaning-making and the uncanniness that comes from larger wholes, finds its most outspoken form in bordering religions, since these exist to protect and maintain the status quo.

If this suggestion holds, the description given of bordering in the Introduction can be tested and amplified, using elements from the playful approach to religion. The bordering attitude towards the phenomena that we just identified as sources of the religious imagination can be considered. The five existential questions mentioned in the Introduction can moreover be assessed for their role in bordering religions.

From the picture that I drew in the Introduction, bordering religions appear in their outspoken form, as ideal types. They are exclusive and self-sufficient in determining their group's meaning-making, and in this sense they are dualist, drawing a clear boundary between "us" and "them," "in" and "out." They are self-assured, allowing themselves to ignore inconvenient questions posed by outsiders. Alternatives are not to be entertained. As we noted, religious diversity does not create worries. Critical questions, such as those raised in the God Debate, are often excluded. Similarly, questions about the role that power mechanisms play in the bordering community are disregarded. The bordering religion's role in both causing and solving global problems does not receive attention. In all these respects, there is an effective check on the believers' meaning-making.

The various sources that were discussed in the previous sections can be found to nourish bordering religions. In fact, any religion that maintains its exclusivity, confirms the theory. I will discuss each of the sources mentioned above in the same order as before.

When bordering religions deal with the basic source of religion, *playful reflection*, they potently reduce the immense amount of signification, taming it and making it benign. The religious adventure is forbidden, "home sweet home" is the rule. Playfulness is eradicated in favor of unambiguous views. Wild reflection is efficiently domesticated. Security is maximized, risk minimized. The view that is selected from the multitude of possibilities as the best one has the advantage that the inexpressible is on speaking terms again. Communication with the sacred is reestablished, in an idiosyncratic manner. The image of the Other is narrowly defined. Control is regained. Instead of loneliness, a feeling of belonging prevails, in close connection with the sacred Other, but also with the community of fellow believers.

Knowledge, time, and space are domains that bordering religions bring under control, also using them as metaphorical repertoires. They may be linked with each other, knowledge about time and space being an important part of the bordering perspective. *Knowledge* is circumscribed and made evident. A selection is made from the unlimited reservoir of meanings. Doctrinal, mythical, and ritual themes are important elements, sometimes elaborated in such a detailed manner that lifelong study is required, coupled with the exclusive role of the religious specialist. The intricacies of religious knowledge may demand the creation of a hierarchy, possibly linked with age. In view of the control that bordering religions exercise over their members, all sectors and aspects of life are covered by the authorized knowledge that is selected. Alternatives are either ignored or strongly criticized. Education disseminates the official versions. A power structure guarantees implementation and sanctions deviation. Thus the religion's views on, for instance, the way the world or human beings emerged, can compete with scientific versions of that event.

The origin of humans and their world also forms an example of the way *time* is approached, mirroring the bordering views and goals. This may also refer to the way believers are supposed to use their time, how ritual time is distinguished, how the history of mankind and the earth is viewed, and how the history of the religion is written. The disturbing limitless nature of time, with its open beginning and end, is domesticated by the idea of eternity and the eternal Other. Transitions in time may be understood as needing special ritual treatment. This may refer to transitions in the course of the day or on the year's calendar, but also to the stages in a believer's life, from birth to death.

In a similar way the bordering perspective influences the notion of *space*, disguising its alarming endlessness. Significantly the bordering metaphor is a spatial one, corresponding with exclusive access to special properties of the sacred, transcending the limits that humans are bound by. In social space, there is a demarcation between insiders and outsiders. Ritual space, in the open air, or in buildings, also expresses the bordering tendency, only enabling access to insiders, or privileged access to an exclusive class of religious specialists. Different bordering religions may make claims on the same place, as is the case of Ayodhya (India) but also of Northern Ireland or Jerusalem. Bordering may lead to the establishment of a territory, reserved for the unique use of believers, a Holy Land. The claim may have historical associations, thereby linking space with time. This may lead to conflicts over territorial claims and the use of violence in the name of the sacred.

Nature is another religious source that believers may interpret in a bordering manner. Borders exist in nature and invite symbolic interpretation. Rivers and transitions in the landscape, for instance, deserts, or beaches, the space between land and sea, feature widely here. The top of a mountain may be viewed as being closest to the sacred, symbolizing the contact between humans and the sacred. Volcanoes are a special case, as are earthquakes. Waterfalls may also inspire religious metaphor. The transition from the inhabited world to unpopulated nature may receive special emphasis. Nature may be associated with the sacred, culture and the inhabited world with sin. Believers may venture into nature to seek a special call or vision, especially when nature is viewed as a sacred domain. The margins may be of great importance and therefore nature can provide the metaphoric repertoire that threatens the center's hegemony. Nature may in contrast also be viewed as wild and profane, as an impossible habitat for the sacred. Monotheist religions especially tend to desacralize nature, making it completely accessible, God-given, and open to human exploration.

In the bordering context, the *body* may serve as the metaphor for the general disciplining that takes place. The stronger the bordering process, the more outspoken the views on the body. This may lead to the use of clothes as a way of distinguishing believers from non-believers. Hierarchical relations can also be expressed in clothing, just as views on gender relations can be shown in this way. Difference may also be established in the ways in which body hair is treated. There may be different expectations for women and men, and men and women may be required to distinguish themselves from each other as well. The rejection of other possibilities in the here and now may lead to an emphasis on the hereafter, as the promised domain, putting the soul above the body. Interpretations of illness and death will match such a perception of the body. Sexuality is often reduced to the reproductive function. The body may be seen as sinful. The way that children are socialized to accept a particular understanding of the body illustrates this. The human body and the body social mirror each other.[30] The apostle Paul invoked the metaphor: "For the body is not one member, but many."[31]

If the *self* in the modern perception is the authentic and free subject, its individuality may be experienced as a rehabilitation of the wild reflection that is proper to the human animal. Bordering religions tend to be critical of the modernization process that made the self its figurehead. Accordingly, the room for self-understanding will be limited and standards will be applied that restrict reflection on the self. Autonomy will not be considered a virtue. The roaming self will be offered asylum in the safe haven of the bordering religion. Those who have difficulty in dealing with the abundant meaning-making of our era will enjoy the security and predictability of this worldview home.

For the bordering religion, *society* is the counterpoint, needed to establish its own contrasting identity, unless a society has been established that respects bordering values. In view of the radical changes that have occurred in modern society, the contrast has deepened. The mini-society of the bordering religious group conditions its members, reinstating the functions of society that, as we saw, correspond in a striking manner to the characteristics attributed to God. The modern autonomous individual is subdued again, the group retaining its pre-modern supra-individual status. Especially when maintaining border control, the group serves as an alternative society, a blueprint for what society should be. This may take the form of a theocratic position, the ideal society experiencing divine rule. Yet, less outspoken forms are also possible.

Then there are the man-made wholes that are experienced as being bigger than the believer. Here as well the bordering mechanisms are active.

---

30. For a classic study, see Douglas, *Natural Symbols*. Also, Synnott, *The Body Social*.
31. 1 Cor 12:14.

In bordering religions *communication*, especially in its modern forms, may be viewed as a threat to the integrity of the group. Part of the border control involves censorship of the available information. This may bar access to modern forms of communication. In some cases bordering religions themselves become active in using mass media as a mode of proselytizing, as in the electronic churches, but also in an effort to inform the adherents in a controlled way. In general, bordering religions have their own forms of communication, serving the values and structures of the group.

Evil was another of the human additions to the experiences of what transcends human will and radius of action, especially in relation to its victims. Bordering religions usually have a clear understanding of what is evil, since anything that deviates from its worldview is labeled as such. This may be reflected in the pantheon, devilish and demonic figures representing evil. In this respect bordering religions may also emphasize duality. Strict morals are often part of the bordering perspective, including an outspoken notion of what is evil. Insiders may thereby mark as evil that which outsiders would not characterize in the same way. Inversely, the bordering group's leadership may endorse views as sound and divinely justified that outsiders would at least frown upon. In relation to the four global problems—poverty, violence, pollution, conflict—bordering religions may play a role that others would regard as negative, especially when the group's interests and its border control demand the use of means that only worsen the situation. This may particularly be the case where violence and conflict are concerned, obviously reinforcing each other.

As far as *music* is concerned, bordering religions have made their contribution to music history, inspiring and generating compositions that served to underline the exclusive identity of the bordering group. Whether a Te Deum, a battle hymn, mantra singing, or revival songs, music can be put to use when demarcating the border of the group, translating doctrine into sound and lyrics. In its ritual function, music can be the mainstay of border identity. In terms of style and performance, music in the bordering context can be both inclusive and exclusive, experienced as either attractive or repulsive.

Consumerism was also included in the man-made experiences of the beyond. When bordering religions are critical of modernization, their criticism may include a reference to consumerism and possibly the market. The dragon may be identified and combatted. The bordering community may develop its own life-style patterns, corresponding to its sub-culture. Yet, consumerism may also be a non-issue, not selected as part of the repertoire that rules the group's bordering policies, and not recognized as relevant to the maintenance of the group.

Finally I presented *religion* itself as a source above and beyond believers, confirming the effect of the other sources. Since bordering religions represent the most outspoken type of religious groups, their case serves as the best example of the impact that a religion can have, confirming the influence of all the other sources mentioned. Once founded, a religion may develop bordering characteristics, establishing itself as an institution, marked by clear structures and obvious borders. In view of what I presented as a theory of religion, bordering religions serve as the clearest example of the theory. As shown in this section, the various sources come together in a constellation. Bordering is their striking characteristic.

In view of the discussion about the relationships between the various sources and the bordering phenomenon, bordering religions can be said to use these sources to provide clear answers to the five ultimate questions mentioned in the Introduction. Bordering religions exploit this potential to the maximum. Moreover, they may be in such a powerful position that they can use these sources for their own ends, colonizing them, interpreting them in their own manner, by making a selective use of their metaphoric repertoires. Thereby each bordering religion compensates for feelings of powerlessness and harnesses the repertoires that the sources represent. The wild imagination is tamed, yet gives heteronyms to the sacred, each bordering religion adopting its own selection, following from its own tastes and interests. In the process, the playful side of religion is easily sacrificed on the altar of the bordering religion.

Conclusion

Another thread in the book's argument, this chapter showed how religion compensates for the shortcomings in the human animal's outfit. The portrait of the human animal provided in the previous chapter proved helpful to understanding a series of characteristics of religion, all included in the checklist for theorists of religion. Both the overwhelming human reflexive capacity and the experience of transcending wholes were presented as sources of religion, also explaining its specificity, functions, and structures. The playful approach to religion was shown to offer an interpretation of these and other aspects of religion. In addition, the bordering process could be included in this approach, since it helps domesticate wild reflection. The chapter thus served as an elaboration of the preliminary exploration of religion presented in chapter one, taking advantage of the views on the human animal developed in chapter two. The notions of power and play, previously introduced, need to be explored further. This exploration will form the basis of the next two chapters.

Forbidden Fruit: 2

Heaven is what I cannot reach!
The apple on the tree,
Provided it do hopeless hang,
That "heaven" is to me.

The color on the cruising cloud,
The interdicted ground
Behind the hill, the house behind, –
There Paradise is found!

—*Emily Dickinson*

four

Powerful Religion

A Sequel

IF GARCÍA MÁRQUEZ WERE an anthropologist—which in a way he was—he might have continued the story with which chapter one began in the following way.

The Esteban stories that people tell make a saint out of a drowned giant. One fisherman starts carving small statue icons out of driftwood. In homes where such statues adorn the house altar, the first miracles are reported. When children play in a dry field just outside the village, a spring bursts forth. The water is said to have healing power. After some months a small chapel is erected on the spot where Esteban's body was thrown over the cliffs. Esteban's statue is given a central position on the altar. The anchor that the men initially had tied to Esteban's bier is placed as a cross on the chapel wall. People come regularly to the chapel to pray.

When more miracles are reported, people from other villages come to the chapel as well. Soon the sanctuary becomes a site for pilgrimage. Especially on weekends, buses and trucks bring pilgrims to Esteban's village. Pilgrims sing the dirge that the women improvised during his wake. Each pilgrim brings a small bier bearing a statue of St. Esteban. Between the bier and the statue are hidden small notes, on which are written requests for help. These mini-biers are thrown off the cliff. Exactly a year after his funeral, Esteban's saint's day is held for the first time, and a procession is led be someone carrying Esteban's statue. Fishing ships immortalize his memory at sea.

The changes in the village capture the attention of the priest who comes to the fishermen's village twice a year to say mass, marry couples, and baptize newborn babies. He reports the events to his bishop, who sends a priest and a nun to offer pastoral care to the pilgrims. The church pays for the erection of a huge statue of St. Esteban at the entrance to the village. On St. Esteban's Day, the bishop himself comes to the chapel to say an open-air mass and to lead the procession. In his sermon, he refers to the sea as the symbol of chaos, to the ship as a symbol of the church, to St. Peter as a fisher of men, and to St. Esteban, the New Testament martyr St. Stephen. The people hardly listen. They came to seek a miracle.

Once the pilgrimage influences daily life, politicians become interested. At election time they are conspicuously present. During the annual procession, they are the bishop's guests on the boat carrying St. Esteban's statue. They emphasize that, thanks to them, the road to the village has been asphalted. They have also invested government money in upgrading the fishing port into a marina.

Some of the fishermen in the village understand the scope of opportunity brought to their corner of the world by the new era that began with Esteban. They open souvenir shops selling Esteban statues and holy spring water. Restaurants open, where "Esteban's fish" is the best-selling dish on the menu. Entrepreneurs using machines have taken the place of the first sculptor. They, in turn, are put out of business when plastic statues are sold with labels that say in small print "Made in China." After some time, the first hotel is opened, quickly followed by an apartment complex. Two years later, a casino is built. Travel agencies organize brief excursions in fishing boats, which by now are no longer used to catch fish. Holidays in Esteban's village are advertised in the national newspapers and weeklies, which boast that the village offers an unparalleled combination of beauty, tradition, and leisure.

Only the women who were present at the wake remember the extraordinary experience that the body of the handsomest drowned man in the world brought to their lives.[1]

---

1. This section is reprinted from Droogers, "The Recovery of Perverted Religion," 24, 25.

Power

The sequel shows how power comes to play a role in the fishermen's village. Earlier, I defined power as the human capacity to influence other people's behavior, even against their will. In a way this is already a rather specific definition, since a minimal definition of power is the capacity to make something happen. The healing power of the water from Esteban's source is an example of this minimal concept. In the social sciences, relations between people are the object of study, which makes it necessary to be more precise with regard to what change is brought about: a change in behavior. "Behavior" should be read here in the broadest sense, and include what people say and even what they think. In social contexts, the use of power means that the number of alternative behaviors is reduced. Therefore power is used as an instrument to curb the immense potential of human reflection, a necessary measure, as was discussed in chapter two.

The inclusion of "even against their will" in the definition of power suggests that the behavioral change that power may bring about need not be the result of consent. Consequently there must be a special reason why people, though they disagree with it, nevertheless do what authority demands of them. The key to the ruler's success is that he controls significant kinds of power that are not accessible to all. Depending on the context, these relatively scarce instruments of power might include money, specialized knowledge, degrees, titles, age, parentage, experience, laws, custom, personal charisma, weapons, or mineral wealth. Wherever leadership plays a role, access to power is unequally distributed and thereby limited. Power may be the privilege of the happy few—who sometimes find themselves rather unhappy when burdened with power. The uneven distribution also harbors the risk of change. New conditions may offer opportunities to new rulers.

Yet, when sufficiently anchored within power structures, any protest against the ruling structure becomes unthinkable. Rulers often use their power to reinforce the conditions that support their power, if necessary creating new means of asserting power, such as via laws. The people whose behavior is controlled by power may accept their humble position as normal. They may even wholeheartedly defend it against possible criticism. Yet, as human beings do not lose the capacity for reflection, in the undercurrent of the group or society, a counter-stream may develop. This force may be invisible but may also be the potential beginning of changing patterns. Besides, good leadership leaves room for individual initiatives. It may even be part of daily practice that people have their own strategies for dealing with those in power, if necessary saying yes outwardly, but inwardly refusing to behave in a particular way. Even under absolute dictatorship human meaning-making can be creative in avoiding imposed behavior patterns. Power is never a simple matter of either all or nothing, despite the popular wisdom that the winner takes it all. The question is much more about the extent to which a person's behavior can be influenced.

Implicit in the above definition of power is the idea that power is an integral part of any set of social relations. Taking the connection between two people, couples, as the minimal model, both partners will in some way influence the other person's behavior. Even the most harmonious relationship is not power-free. Harmony only means that the participants mutually accept the way their behavior is influenced by the others. Commonly, power is only used as a term when there is a conflict through which people become aware of the ways in which their autonomy is compromised or subjugated. This has contributed to the negative connotation that the term carries, and it is why power is sometimes labeled as "dirty." Accordingly, rulers sometimes deny that they have power or relativize their influence.

To gain a better understanding of the way power is used, a distinction can be made between self-serving and subservient power and rulers. *Self-serving* rulers transform their power from a means into a goal in itself, with the intention of maintaining their own power, whatever the other goals are that their authority is supposed to serve. Their power is then presented as necessary and natural. *Subservient* rulers, in contrast, use their power to facilitate the realization of goals other than their own power interests. They will lose their power if they do not succeed in realizing these goals. It must be added that any form of power needs minimal conditions to function and will as a consequence seek to guarantee these conditions. Yet, subservient power is easily transformed into self-serving power. The main purpose of drawing this distinction is to highlight the moment at which concrete power switches from being subservient to self-serving. Dictators are experts in self-serving power, though they will always disguise what they do with a discourse of subservient power.

Power and Religion

As far as power is concerned, religions represent a special case, because next to human power sacred power is involved. Let us first consider sacred power. The relationship between believers and the sacred is crucial to perspectives on power in a religion. The extraordinary form of supernatural power forms the essence of religion, reflecting the transcendental "beyond" that serves as religion's source, reflected in the experience of greater wholes that exceed human control. A major power that overarches and covers the human power constellation in a religion can be sensed. Accordingly, the sacred Other is often spoken of in terms of power. Both internally and in its external relations, a religion adopts a perspective on divine power that will correspond with—or at least not contradict—its own power structure. Bordering religions show this connection in an outspoken way.

Believers are convinced that the divine constantly influences their behavior, which is what power does in terms of the aforementioned definition. However, they may find it difficult to express this sensation. Metaphors taken from profane human power contexts—such as Lord, King, kingdom, Master, submission, dependence—are the only means available to communicate the nature of divine power. Military symbolism may play a role as well, as when terms such as victory and surrender are used, reflecting the way divine power is thought to operate, especially in a dualist perspective. Like the earthly rulers, God or the gods may punish believers, just as they may reward them. They may wage a war. The use of the symbolism of human power colors the image of the divine power that a religion defends.

As suggested by the definition of power offered, believers may experience divine influence on their behavior as making them act against their own will. It is common for religious founders to resist their vocation. Conversion stories often refer to initial resistance. Negative sanctions commonly go against the believer's will and understanding. In other cases however, such as in prayer and sacrifice, believers ask for divine intervention in their life and can't wait for it to arrive.

The distinction between subservient and self-serving power can not only be applied to human relations, but also to the believer's relation with the sacred, or perhaps on a personal level, the divine. Bordering religions, focused as they are on border maintenance, with a tendency to self-serving power, will probably describe the divine in terms of their own preoccupations. In any case, power takes a central place as soon as metaphors from human power relations are used to characterize the experience of sacred power. Once a religion has developed a set of secular power metaphors that apply to the divine, the human and divine will tend to reinforce each other.

The bordering phenomenon can therefore become rather persistent and resilient, having roots in society and culture.

However, much depends on the concepts of the divine that religions develop. As we saw, an important criterion to distinguish between the two types of power is the degree to which the exercise of power is self-maintaining, keeping the ruler and the system that he represents in place. In view of the fact that divine power reflects human experiences with phenomena that are beyond human control, sacred power is thought to be sufficient in itself, unquestioned, always and anywhere the same, just as the image of the more extreme forms of human power. Accordingly, strong borders come with outspoken power metaphors.

Believers may view this power as subservient, but they often give it self-serving traits. A case in point is the way in which believers accept their toil and affliction as divinely given. God is, for example, supposed to teach them a lesson. In the Christian context, and depending on the type of theology, Jesus' suffering may be viewed as a model, suggesting that a person may suffer as a form of atonement, or for the greater glory of the almighty God. Whether human or divine, absolute power cannot be questioned. This conviction legitimates both human and divine self-serving power.[2]

In addition to sacred power, any religion contains human power. Like every human group, a religious organization functions thanks to power mechanisms. Believers are not always aware that this is the case, especially as long as things go smoothly. Bordering tendencies may in this sense be experienced as natural and normal. Moreover, religious views often emphasize the equality of all believers before the sacred, thereby ignoring the role of power in differentiating between people. Power will therefore ideally more often be presented as being subservient, and in fact all religions defend some view on the desired quality of life, elaborating this in terms of values and norms that must prevent the abuse of power. Nevertheless, self-serving power may reach the stage that it justifies the taking of human lives, both in killing opponents and in sacrificing one's own life for the sake of one's religion, as modern religious terrorism has made tragically clear, 9/11 being the most dramatic case. Self-serving power may be pushed to the point that the core values of its own religion are ignored.

---

2. For an analysis of the role of power in the history of Christianity, see Lenoir, *Le Christ philosophe*. Lenoir illustrates, without using the distinction, how the subservient elements in Christianity were constantly perverted by the church as a self-serving institution. See also Ellul, *La subversion du christianisme*.

In looking at instruments of power, religions form a particular example. Specialized knowledge, tradition, age, charisma, titles, and religious experience may be relatively more important instruments of power in religious, compared with non-religious, contexts. An institution in the religious field has the unique possibility—absent in purely secular contexts—to appeal to the divine order when seeking to justify its own power. The sacred thus becomes an instrument of power. Especially power of the self-serving kind may make use of this legitimating technique, whereas the subservient type does not need such a strategy because it is justified by its serving and facilitating role. Paradoxically, divine subservient power may be recruited in the service of self-serving religious rulers, who may reinforce their position by acting as spokespersons for the sacred entity, or at least as inspired authorized interpreters of the core message. Institutionalization and exclusivity go hand in hand.

An important element in the exercise of religious power is control over access to the sacred as an instrument of power. Differences in this respect may be legitimated by reference to divine intervention, a special vocation, a mystical ability, a healing capacity, or some extraordinary experience, any of which distinguish one believer from all others. Besides, exclusive knowledge—of rituals, or holy scriptures and their language, or of religious law books—may serve as an instrument of power. Tradition is often a guarantee for continuity in the distribution of power.

Most religions have a class of religious specialists who behave as proprietors of the religion and as keepers of the pure and true faith. This class may be organized in a hierarchical way, thereby differentiating between levels of power. Usually its members are liberated from other tasks to exercise their religious work for at least part of their time. They do not take part in the economic production process, yet derive income by producing religious services. The bordering process may demand an elaborated division of labor, even within the class of religious specialists, tasks being defined by the need for border maintenance.

Religious and secular power can coincide, just as they may reinforce each other, the secular rulers putting their mode of power at the disposal of the sacred rulers, the latter legitimating secular power by sacred means. In Christianity, this has been the case since Constantine (272–337 AD). The net result is that religious and secular leaderships put limits on alternative behavior and thereby to religious as well as secular change.

However, religious and secular powers may also be in constant competition, seeking to influence the behavior of the same people, but in different ways. In the Investiture Contest, pope and emperor disputed each other's right to nominate bishops and abbots for a long time (the pope won, greatly strengthening his power). Henry VIII (1491–1547) is a special case of a secular ruler who, adopting a self-serving style of power, created a religious counter-institution to serve his private interests. The end of the German Democratic Republic and the fall of the Berlin Wall were, in part, the consequence of the Protestant Church's campaign for more freedom. In Poland, around the same time, the Catholic Church played a similar role.

In any religion, and despite the best of intentions, the seductions of self-serving power may be real, though not always consciously understood. This type of power will be legitimated by reference to some form of divine inspiration. A reform movement may contest such a self-serving power system, including its self-legitimation. In the history of the Catholic Church, monastic orders have often been found to play this critical role. Initially they operated from the margin, but gradually many moved to the center. The changing social context may create new demands for a religious institution. This happened during the Reformation, accompanying, and in reaction to, profound changes in society. It led to new institutions, with a variety of power structures, from egalitarian Quakers, via the Presbyterian type of so-called "democratic churches," to episcopal churches and hierarchical state churches.

Whatever the power system at work in a religion, the material dimension will reflect it, for example, in the architecture of temples and church buildings. Possibly in this sense it mirrors secular power. The stronger the power structure, the more visible its material manifestation. Bordering religions may be recognized by their material presence in public space. The arrangement of the inner space of temples and the use of furniture may express the power distinction between clergy and laity, as is obvious in Catholic churches, but also in several Pentecostal churches, once they become more institutionalized.

In general, as standardized religious behavior, ritual will mirror the power constellation.[3] The fact that ritual has the connotation of being unchangeable and fixed points to its role in the continuation of religious power. The more complex a ritual is, the more believers depend on the ritual specialists' expertise. In terms of the definition of power at work

3. Bell, *Ritual Theory, Ritual Practice,* especially Part III.

here, during the ritual, the specialist has the right and capacity to influence the behavior of other believers. His status may require that he wear special clothes, speak an expert language, and have exclusive access to certain parts of the religious space. The consumption of food offerings may be his privilege.

To understand religious processes of power, it is useful to look at how a religious movement emerges and how it develops into an established religion. Often the founder is more of a charismatic religious virtuoso than a bureaucratic organizer. He (or she) is interested in divine power, not his own. Usually being marginal to established religion, he enjoys the freedom to explore new experiences and insights—as long as he is left alone. His position in the margin distinguishes him from the religious power center of his day. He may have some difficulty in telling others about his inspiring experience with the sacred, being more a miracle-doer than a speaker, more a stammering eccentric than a rhetorical genius. Commonly relationships in an early phase of a religious movement are fairly horizontal, with strong feelings of solidarity and *communitas*.[4]

But such a movement will attract people. The ensuing enthusiasm may be so great that conversion to the new message becomes a goal of the movement. Conversion is a form of the exercise of power, since the converter seeks to influence the convert's behavior. The size of the membership is a power base. Subsequently success must be managed. The need for an organizer is felt, somebody who is able to direct masses and translate the inchoate inspirations of the founder into a clear proselytizing message. Along with Moses, an Aaron is needed; a Jesus is followed by a Peter or a Paul; after a Mohammed comes an Abu Bakr.

The rise of the movement may provoke a strong reaction from the established clergy, who may experience the new competitor as a threat to their power, leading them to persecute the believers of the new movement. Yet, in the course of time, the newcomer may come to replace the former persecutor, usually after a fierce power struggle, often involving secular power in addition to religious power.

Once successful, within one or two generations, the movement will slow down and become an institution. Bordering tendencies may then begin to manifest themselves. Institutionalization will also bring with it the tendency to influence the surrounding society. Once established, the new religion will become aware of the power of its message and will want

4. Turner, *Ritual Process*.

to change society accordingly. Its message may contain views on the ideal society.

From the margin, the new religion moves to the center. In the process, there may be a shift from subservient to self-serving power. A justification is easily found, often with arguments that stem from the field of subservient language. Out of neighborly love, that neighbor must be coerced to join, for her or his salvation and benefit. The religion's leader will easily pose as the *primus inter pares*. The deeper the institutionalization, the greater the chance that self-serving power will interdict subservient power. If an alliance with secular power is established, that process will accelerate. If the self-serving nature of power can no longer be denied, the cycle will make a fresh start, with a religious virtuoso calling for a return to subservient values. If successful, after a few generations, the movement will be part of the institutionalized center, with new dissidents to save the pure message from contamination.

The dynamics of these power processes seem to be sociological in nature, but they may have theological consequences. The way in which the concept of God is defined may be influenced by the interests of the leaders, especially in contexts where self-serving power dominates. The metaphors used to describe the nature of this God, may reflect the clergy's views on power, including the significance of their own position. As I suggested already, the secular repertoire for metaphors of power may furnish complementary and effective images. Secular power symbolism contaminates religious views on sacred power. State churches may exemplify this process. Generally speaking, the profane power model that the religious leaders adopt will color their view of God. When, in the previous chapter, we discussed society as a source for the religious experience, we saw how God and society may share important characteristics. This will, of course, hugely influence leaders to adopt the power terminology of society. Other repertoires, including those containing meanings that would be in keeping with the views of the religion's origins and founder—for example, those emphasizing compassion, vulnerability,[5] service or even powerlessness—are easily ignored in daily practice, since they do not support self-serving power. They may nevertheless be part of the discourse that keeps the system in place.

---

5. McGilchrist, *The Master and His Emissary*, 384, calls the vulnerability of the divine the core *mythos* of Christianity.

Although theological reflection is conscious *per se*, it also depends on the spontaneous and intuitive selection of concepts, metaphors, and meanings. Theologians are not always aware of all aspects of this process. Knowledge is conditioned. This is even more so the case with popular religions. Popular religion may be a precursor of official religion, especially when elements of it are integrated into official practice or doctrine, as was the case with the Maria cult and the saints in Catholicism. The capacity to adopt particular aspects of other perspectives may be part of a self-serving strategy.

Whether used in official or in popular religion, the vocabulary of power creeps smoothly into worldview. The distinction itself is, of course, a symptom of differences in power within the religious division of labor. The power schema, with all its connotations, may predominate, even if the believers suffer the consequences of that schema, for example, by having to make personal sacrifices. They may do so without protest, even on their own initiative. Paradoxically the same power schema may offer compensation via discourse, by transferring the locus of the power from humans to the divine, thereby lessening the believers' suffering.

René Girard[6] has developed an interesting approach to religion and power, though it is not without speculative elements. In his view, humans are ruled by mimetic desire, wanting what their neighbor has, contrary to the idea that each person is authentic in his or her desires. Sharing the same desire causes envy, creates conflicts, and stimulates the use of violence. People seek to exercise power over each other. Religion serves to control violence and to compensate for frustration. It does so, according to Girard, by applying the scapegoat mechanism. Collective anger, the consequence of the unfulfilled desire, is directed against one person. Desire is no longer shared, and instead, aggression is the common characteristic. By eliminating the scapegoat, peace is restored. But having served as the cause of renewed harmony, the scapegoat obtains a sacred status, with special powers. Ritual sacrifice repeats the original event, but this time emphasizing restored harmony. Taboos surround the objects once desired by all. Myths are narratives of the scapegoat's end and rehabilitation. Ultimately mimetic desire nourishes and legitimates the status quo of mechanisms of power and curbs free meaning-making. In my view, it can be added to the list of the wholes, discussed in chapter three, that are beyond human control and that serve as sources for religion, thereby restoring control. It shows the

6. Williams, *Girard Reader.*

human animal's difficulty in managing his or her meaning-making ability. The scapegoat mechanism can be understood as part of the effort to regain control over what seemed beyond human control. In an interview, Girard added neoteny to his theory, suggesting that the effort to restore harmony is necessary to guarantee the premature child's survival.[7]

On foundations laid by prophets, priests build their temples, synagogues, cathedrals, and mosques. They establish their canons of meanings, scriptures, rituals, and doctrines. The key concepts and symbols are their domain. The founder's religiosity becomes the priests' religion. Prose is a substitute for poetry, law replaces tentative advice, doctrine takes the place of worldview experiments, the central institution excludes the marginal movement, and self-serving tendencies override subservient religion. Until one day, a prophet stands up to speak . . . .

Power in Esteban's Story

Márquez's story and my sequel to it can be reread in light of this discussion of power. The gender order determines the distribution of power, although at a certain point the women succeed in determining men's behavior, inverting the status quo. The fact that their experience with the drowned man is of a religious nature, temporarily increases their power. The power they attribute to Esteban is religious, which legitimates their actions. The women can be viewed as the architects of the new cult, who impose it on the village. Taking advantage of the margins that the event brings with it, they freely explore its possible meanings. Everything seems possible when their imagination seizes power. They feel overwhelmed as well as empowered by the event. All previous experiences of failure in those areas of life that were beyond their control are transformed and inverted by clothing the corpse, not only in his shroud, but in a whole series of characteristics that could be used to define Esteban's sacred power.

In the sequel, the rise of Esteban's cult is accompanied by changes in the religious, political, and economic realms. A powerful saint, he attracts not only devout pilgrims, but also followers, traditional or new, from the village or elsewhere, who consider themselves stakeholders in the new cult and thus in the local power hierarchy. Though all will pose as devotees of St. Esteban, all have their own agenda regarding the distribution of power, whether religious, economic, or political. What to the women seemed a

7. Müller, "Interview with René Girard."

deep religious experience becomes a commodity with an economic value. In this sense, Esteban's influence is not limited to the field of popular religion. A new constellation of power relations has emerged, with a fair chance that not all types of power are of the subservient type. The closed world of the village is substituted with the open global world. Especially the men, the clergy, the entrepreneurs, and the politicians will tend to maintain their power, if necessary crossing the border between subservient and self-serving power. Some of the witnesses of the extraordinary events will serve from time to time as guardians of collective memory, correcting false versions and recalling the true origin of the cult.

How Power Rules Religion

Power has so far been presented as a necessary element in social life, and in religion. Since people influence each other's behavior, power is inevitable. Power in itself is neutral, but it can be used in both a subservient and a self-serving way. The machinations of power in the religious context will be explored further here. In this section, I will first show how two typical elements in the religious context—the scarce nature of the founding religious experience and the difficulty of telling others about it—help to put power on a pedestal. Then, in the next section, I will describe how the same religious characteristics can also curb power. Power may rule religion, but religion is also able to curb power.

The first characteristic of power to be discussed here is the effect of the scarce nature of religious experiences. Personal religious life-changing events, offering deep insights into existential questions, are not evenly distributed. Just as not everyone is musically gifted, religious abilities are a singular gift. However, most people can fully appreciate the religious dimension, just as there are many more people who love music than there are musicians. As suggested above, a religious movement starts in the margin of a society with a religious virtuoso, say a Buddha, a Jesus, a Mohammed, or more recently a Joseph Smith, a Simon Kimbangu, or a Bhagwan Shree Rajneesh. The margin makes the virtuoso's experience seem exceptional. He may have difficulty in recognizing the special and exceptional nature of this experience, or in accepting the consequences of it. Uncertainty and doubt may keep him from taking any initiative.

Though so far I have used the male form, the virtuoso can also be a woman, a Hildegard von Bingen, a Mary Baker Eddy, or an Aimee Semple

McPherson. In fact, the marginal position that women usually occupy may coincide with extraordinary religious experiences—experiences that deviate from the mainstream repertoire controlled from the male-dominated center. In chapter one, I referred to the relationship between women and the margin. From the very beginnings of Esteban's cult, the women were instrumental. As a result of their marginal status, women are also often among the first followers of a new movement.

Whether a man or a woman, the virtuoso is the owner, willy-nilly, of a scarce resource, and this serves as an instrument of power. The extraordinary event gives the person who experienced it a special status. Such a person draws attention. She (or he) may come to be viewed as an intermediary between the sacred and the human, but it is also possible that she is taken to be a source of sacred power herself. This may take the concrete form of healihg abilities, drawing in many people who seek help. Straight away or gradually, the scarce nature of the founding experience makes the virtuoso the founder of a new movement.

All then depends on the founder's reaction to the new status. The subservient/self-serving dilemma may become a real problem, discouraging or stimulating bordering tendencies. Other persons will adopt leading roles, controlling the scarce spiritual good. Thus the foundations are laid for the power dynamics in the movement. The new leadership will tend to control access to the sacred, to the founder, and to power positions. Whether the scarce nature of the religious product will be maintained, depends very much on the vicissitudes of a movement's history and the eventual bordering process. The trend may be towards subservient as well as to self-serving power, to inclusivity and exclusivity.

If scarcity acted as an impetus for power mechanisms to start operating, a second impetus will emerge soon after. The religious product is not only scarce, it is also difficult to sell, explain, and understand. In converting new adherents to the movement, believers encounter difficulties in communicating the core message. Since the sacred stems from somewhere beyond human understanding and is called forth by a lack of human comprehension, it does not fit the common categories of interpretation, particularly if it is revealed by a totally new experience. Experiences of the sacred will invite wild reflection, a constant testing of images and meanings, of narratives and gestures. The founder may be an outstanding religious virtuoso, yet if he (or she) has to tell others about his religious experience, he may find this an impossible task. If a vision or a dream was his founding experience, how can he tell others about it? One method may be to offer a striking symbol, taken from that vision or dream. It may involve using more than a thousand words, especially when evoking a bodily experience. Even then opinions may differ as to the meanings of the symbol. The path in Buddhism and the cross in Christianity are strong symbols, yet they have been interpreted in an diverse range of ways. Meaning-making is a complicated process.

Although the human animal possesses the capacity for language, this asset also has its shortcomings. In telling others about a fundamental religious experience, the gift of speech can be helpful, but it will never be able to fully convey the whole experience. Even gifted writers can only lift a corner of the veil. As the Brazilian poet Mário Quintana put it: "You think something, finally write something else, and the reader understands something else again. . . . In the meantime the so-called thing begins to suspect that it has not been called so."[8] Roland Barthes suggested that language is not characterized by all it makes possible to say, but by what it obliges us to say.[9] He even called language fascistic, thus drawing attention to its role in power processes. It is a social phenomenon and the fact that it has to serve both communication and power interests necessarily reduces its potential. Any speaker would like to be understood and yet in using language loses depth of meaning. "Text tells lies to create truth," as Lynda Sexson put it.[10] Religious language, being called on to explain the sacred secret, always mystifies. It is more poetic than prosaic.

The difficulty of communicating a core experience opens the door to power, since it gives some people the opportunity to use their verbal and rhetorical capacity in order to become the spokespersons for a movement and its founder. The movement takes leave of its stammering first formulations and starts looking for unequivocal formulations. The spokesperson distills the inchoate repertoire from the first stage of the movement into a clear message that can be distributed via simple slogans and attractive phrases. Moreover, the process of meaning-making can start to be undertaken in a systematic way, codifying the stories, creating a canon of rituals, and establishing a doctrine. The first versions of new holy scriptures will begin to circulate. Any contradictions and gaps in the movement's repertoire of narratives, rituals, and ideas will be corrected. New movements

8. Translated from Quintana, *Caderno H,* 54.

9. Barthes, *Oevres Complètes,* 431–32.

10. Sexson, *Ordinarily Sacred,* 30.

leave room to explore the new message for deeper meaning. Everybody selects his own meanings. Since the founder was usually not a rhetorical virtuoso, many interpretations are possible.

However, soon the first conflicts will emerge, with opposing factions defending differing views. The right to formulate the correct version serves as a power base for the spokespersons, but which faction has the right version? As was true of the early centuries of both Buddhism and Christianity, the first councils must be held to decide over conflicting interpretations and versions, therein providing the first authoritative texts and formulations. Movements may split over contested issues, as happened to Islam shortly after it started, separating Shia from Sunni. The Protestant Reformation movement also splintered into a number of sub-movements. And there are numerous other examples, all world religions having their factions and schools. Power struggles are part of this process, with rulers traversing the delicate border between subservient and self-serving power, possibly seeking coalitions with secular rulers. The first schools or modalities emerge, seeking to influence as many believers as possible, in extreme cases labeling others as heretics who deserve to be persecuted or even killed.

The meaning-making process that results in a repertoire has a social dimension, also determined by power mechanisms. The leaders who organize the people around the new message expect the spokespersons to come up with an indisputable version. As a consequence, the organizers and the spokespersons will have to cooperate if they wish to keep their power within the hierarchy. That is how the institutionalization of religion takes place, complete with its own labor division.

The scarce nature of religious experience and the difficulty of communicating that experience, point to a paradox in religions that also relates to the transition from a powerful religion (especially in the self-serving sense) to a playful religion. The virtuoso's experience draws from the wild meaning-making game, extracting new symbols and new meanings from the vast range of possibilities. To be able to convey this precious find, it must be reduced to a crystal-clear message. Power is a useful tool for introducing people to an intelligible organizational context, just as it organizes them into a new group. The paradox is that religion for its renewal depends on the inchoate playful experience of a few. It also depends on the power that translates the result into an intelligible form. Power transforms the many into a community, in the process often sacrificing its playful origin.

It seems to me that here the distinction between subservient and self-serving power can be useful. Subservient power allows for a margin to develop in which free meaning-making is possible, guaranteeing some form of continuity, while also remaining aware of the risk of a changeover to self-serving power. The distinction also points to the delicate and sometimes tragic dilemma that religious leaders, in bordering religions, face. Their version of the original founding experience may be as far removed from what really happened as my summary or my sequel to Márquez's story is from the original text. In accepting responsibility for protecting and guarding the core message, as if it were their only child, they risk cuddling it to death once the room enabling wild imagination is closed off.

Christianity, or at least a version of it devised by some of its first canonizers, offers a straightforward image of this paradox: "The Word was made flesh and dwelt among us" (John 1: 14). The sacred cannot be expressed by words, but must become flesh, a living person, in order to be understood. In this revolutionary inversion, the sacred is not rendered adequately via words, but the Word is made into a person of flesh and blood, a human animal. This should leave us speechless.

How Religion Curbs Power

Opportunities for power to be called upon are inherent in religions, as a consequence of the rare nature of the founding experience that remains difficult to explain. Power processes that are part and parcel of any group's practice also apply in religious communities. Despite possessing core values that are meant to govern social life, such as solidarity and compassion, a religious group is no exception to the rule of power. And yet, religion potentially also contains elements that could act as a counterweight to power, especially in its self-serving manifestations. Interestingly, the two characteristics that create scope for power, also reduce its impact. Whereas power can never be abandoned fully, these factors may enlarge the possibilities for the exercise of subservient power. This may be a way out of a sterile bordering process.

First comes the scarce nature of authentic religious experiences. With scarcity comes longing for life-altering, pure, and fundamental experience. In any religion, believers will come to consider the founder's existential experience and insights as the ideal model for their faith. To keep the memory of this alive is a major task for both clergy and laity. It is possible, especially

when self-serving power prevails, that the central leadership impercepti-
bly loses sight of that part of its heritage. Consequently, only those in the
margin can remember why it all began. The leaders' tragic fate is that they
have to organize their religion, but the power mechanisms that are applied
distract them from the original version. This introduces characteristics that
are in the interests of the exercise of power, but do not necessarily confirm
the religion's core values. Secular strategies for an effective set of opera-
tional procedures may come to predominate.

As soon as the developments in a religion culminate in the neglect
of what the founding event stands for, some believers will call for a return
to the source, sometimes after a dramatic event that leads to a person's re-
conversion. The initiative may also come from within the hierarchy, but
then almost always from the lower echelons, as Martin Luther reminds
us. In Márquez's story, Esteban's corpse washed ashore, causing women in
particular to reconsider their understanding of life. Whenever a new version of a story emerges, a fresh formulation of the core religious message,
with a selection of new meanings, will serve as a wake-up call. Playing with
symbols and meanings, long neglected aspects of the original message are
recovered and given a prominent place. Inversion of established rules is
common, as when Jesus and his disciples reaped grain on the Sabbath.[11]
Totally new ideas may also emerge. Bordering tendencies may come under criticism. The exclusivity of an over-institutionalized religion may be
rejected. Clerical leaders may be denounced. It is not a coincidence that
these same elements often go against the self-serving side of power by emphasizing the importance of humility, vulnerability, poverty, sacrifice, and
equality. Revivals, especially in their initial stages, are therefore marked by
subservient power.

Commonly, the leadership, particularly when behaving as self-serving
owners of the institution, will not like this criticism and will tend to label
the countermovement as "sectarian" or "subversive." Even though the dissenters may serve as the religion's memory and conscience, a conflict will
most probably follow, and the outcome will be uncertain. Yet it is also possible that self-serving power is more lenient and will succeed in maintaining itself by integrating elements from the new alternative version, adapting
them in the process of adoption. One visit to Assisi suffices to enable us
to understand what the critique of the humble poverty movement that St.
Francis started has brought forth.

11. Mark 2:23.

The second aspect that creates opportunities for power to establish itself, relates to the difficulty of explaining basic insights. Here too the inverse may occur, principally because concerned believers will feel the need to explore always newer forms of expression. Language can then be rehabilitated, despite its imperfections. Especially poetry, open to multiple interpretations, may compensate for the precise, but limited and domesticated, style of prose in doctrine and law. The rational type of reflection can be complemented with a recovery of the emotion that came with the founding experience and insight. Not only the brain, but the whole body can be sensitized. Mysticism and ecstasy can be given the place they once had. Formal ritual can be transformed by informal experiment. All efforts serve in the communication of the basic views. The religion's repertoires are revitalized. Simultaneously, the dominant image of power and leadership may be changed, especially when subservient values are reinstated. A new repertoire is a challenge to established leadership, especially if the leaders identify with the tradition. Much depends on the way this challenge is dealt with.

The history of most religions contains examples of these reinvigorating efforts, often occurring in a cyclical rhythm. Unless this new form is rejected or marginalized by representatives of self-serving power, the results will be embraced after some time. Possibly even these will come under criticism when the next wave of change occurs. In addition, globalization has opened the possibility of taking elements from other religious contexts and integrating them, as happens when Zen is adopted in Christian monasteries. Globalization has also set the stage for syncretistic compositions of ideas and practices from a variety of backgrounds, as happens in relation to the New Age. Moreover, individuals may use phases of crisis in their lives to find new formulations and practices of faith, adapted to the problem they are confronted with, death being each person's ultimate crisis. Nowadays, elements from religions other than the person's original faith may be included. It is as if the awareness that real wisdom is not easily expressed offers a good reason to open a religion's windows, enabling unknown inspirations from elsewhere to drift in.

Conclusion

Mapping the role of power in the religious landscape, we came across a number of modalities and variations. Bordering was one of them. The distinction between self-serving and subservient power helped us identify a moment in a religion's dealing with power through time. Some of the characteristics that are typical of religion were shown to promote as well as to restrain the effects of power. Thus the dynamics of the relation between religion and power were made visible. In the case of bordering religions, the possibility of change was thus identified. If we add the role of play to the process, as will be done in the next chapter, the route for the transition from a powerful to a playful religion can be surveyed.

The Preacher

He preached upon "breadth" till it argued him narrow, –
The broad are too broad to define;
And of "truth" until it proclaimed him a liar, –
The truth never flaunted a sign.

Simplicity fled from his counterfeit presence
As gold the pyrites would shun.
What confession would cover the innocent Jesus
To meet so enabled a man!

—*Emily Dickinson*

five

Playful Religion

Halfway Score

THE BORDERING PHENOMENON HAS been depicted in this analysis as being rooted in the condition of the human animal who solves the problem of excessive meaning-making by using that selfsame capacity to integrate anything that might propel her or him towards a more or less meaningful way of life. Power was shown to be an ingredient of any religion, bordering being the expression of the leadership's preoccupation with safeguarding identity, both with regard to external contexts and the internal order. Depending on the way power is exercised, bordering religions and religiosity may take several positions on the spectrum between the poles of subservient and self-serving power, with a tendency to self-serving power.

We have now reached the point of the sonnet's caesura in this analysis. The problem of the bordering process has been explored, the map has been drawn, and now we will have to decide how to continue our journey, finding the most efficient path. The direction I suggest is that of play. As far as meaning-making is concerned, the concept of play is oversaturated with meanings. This makes it a tricky term. So my first task will be to discuss the term. In doing so, I will have to show the link with the human animal's outfit. In view of the prominence I give to power in my argument, the connection between play and power must be explored carefully. Few believers would associate their religion with play, and only few scholars studying religion would do so.[1] Accordingly, it is my task to plainly show how religion

---

1. Bellah, *Religion in Human Evolution*; Huizinga, *Homo Ludens*; Turner, *Ritual*

and play can be linked. At this point of my argument, I will introduce the cognitive apparel that makes both play and power possible. Once this is clear, in the chapter's conclusion, the playful approach can be applied to the bordering phenomenon.

Play

Play comes in a huge variety of forms, which makes it difficult to define. I will not even venture to provide a summary of all that play might entail. The term applies to a diverse array of people, such as children, actors, sportspersons, musicians, gamers, and lovers. Not only humans, but even animals play. What could be common to all these instances? And would that leave scope to add believers to the list of playing humans?

The literature on play is as varied as play itself.[2] Many authors take a particular form of play as their topic, or as their starting-point, and then generalize their argument towards a broad definition. The most famous study of play, Johan Huizinga's *"Homo Ludens,"*[3] takes the Middle Ages as a test case, although the book is also in comparative scope. Huizinga provides this synopsis:

> Summing up the formal characteristic of play we might call it a free activity standing quite consciously outside "ordinary" life as being "not serious," but at the same time absorbing the player intensely and utterly. It is an activity connected with no material interest, and no profit can be gained by it. It proceeds within its own proper boundaries of time and space according to fixed rules and in an orderly manner. It promotes the formation of social groupings that tend to surround themselves with secrecy and to stress the difference from the common world by disguise or other means.[4]

Process; Turner, *Anthropology of Performance*.

2. Alexander, "Contribution to the Theory of Play"; Bateson, "A Theory of Play and Fantasy"; Caillois, *Man, Play, and Games*; Caillois, "The Definition of Play"; Cox, *Feast of Fools*; Ehrmann et al., "Homo Ludens Revisited"; Fink, *Spiel als Weltsymbol*; Huizinga, *Homo Ludens*; Clifford Geertz, "Deep Play"; Kinsley, *The Divine Player*; Kliever, "Fictive Religion: Rhetoric and Play"; Miller, *Gods and Games*; Nemoianu and Royal, *Play, Literature, Religion*; Pruyser, *Dynamic Psychology of Religion*; Pruyser, *Play of the Imagination*; Sutton-Smith, *Ambiguity of Play*; Turner, *From Ritual to Theatre*; Winnicott, *Playing and Reality*.

3. Huizinga, *Homo Ludens*.

4. Ibid., 13.

Play appears to be free, outside the ordinary, not taken seriously, yet absorbing, with no material interests, occupying its own time and space, showing order and rules, and surrounded by secrecy. The characteristics that Huizinga selects reflect the medieval context, especially the element of secrecy. Relevant to our topic is that Huizinga sees a connection between play and religion, cult and ritual.[5] Obviously Huizinga, in emphasizing the absence of profit, was writing prior to the current epoch that has commercialized several forms of play, including sports and games, although prizes have been awarded for these activities for centuries. Profit may thus be part of the phenomenon.

The suggestion that play is not taken seriously could be misunderstood,[6] because people, when asked to name the first connotation of the term "play" that comes to mind, would affirm that it is not serious. Yet, the fact that play absorbs the player "intensely and utterly," as Huizinga put it, suggests that the player takes her (or his) play seriously. Otherwise she would be a spoilsport. When Huizinga labels play as "not serious," he does so in comparison to "ordinary" life. The lack of material interest and of profit confirms this. I take seriousness to be an essential element in play. Anyway, when connecting play with religion, the role of seriousness is not at issue, in view of the usual believers' attitude, since the religious game absorbs the believer "intensely and utterly." The problem in suggesting a link is more to do with the popular association of play with what is not serious, or just a game. A child that cannot stand to lose must learn to take his game less seriously. As an adult, he will most probably continue in this practice, denying the serious character of play.

Another approach worth examining is Roger Caillois' study of play in games.[7] Caillois adopts several elements of Huizinga's definition, leaving out secrecy, and adding uncertainty and make-believe. In the literature of play there are other approaches, such as so-called game theory. This represents a specialized field of study, using mathematics and computers, to discover the strategic ways in which people make successful rational choices, including the influence that other people and their choices exert. Another field in which play has a central place, is so-called "serious gaming." This method is used in communicating information, knowledge transfer being

5. Ibid., 20–27.

6. Similar criticism by Ehrman et al., "Homo Ludens Revisited," 33, and Pannenberg, *Anthropologie in theologischer Perspektive*, 323, 324.

7. Caillois, "The Definition of Play," 128.

made effective by engaging participants as players in a game. It is especially used in education, management, health care, and politics.[8]

The definition I propose, admittedly one among many, focuses on a particular characteristic present in many forms of play. To me, play is *the human capacity to deal simultaneously and subjunctively with two or more ways of classifying reality.*[9] The simultaneous presence of two or more realities suggests a "double awareness," as Paul W. Pruyser called it.[10] The term "subjunctively" is taken from Victor W. Turner, who in discussing play, distinguishes between the indicative and the subjective moods, respectively the domain of "as is" and "as if," the latter expressing supposition, desire, possibility, and hypothesis.[11] Most of the instances of play just mentioned meet this definition. Whether children, actors, sportspersons, musicians, gamers, or lovers, all use play to create an absorbing alternative reality, and as Huizinga suggested, are bound to a particular time and place with its own codes and rules, intended for fun or some other form of satisfaction.

Whereas most definitions treat play as a phenomenon with some defining characteristics, I prefer to list play as a human capacity, in the same way that religion, power, and culture can be understood primarily as human abilities. The double orientation that a capacity for play makes possible connects play with the ordinary world, instead of separating it from normal life, as Huizinga does. In my view, the essence of play cannot be understood without recognizing this inbuilt dualism. In this way, humans are depicted as tending to divide their world in opposing directions, playing with the contrasts. Even when they opt for monism, the dual perspective is included, albeit as a negation.

Play and Power

Power was defined earlier in this analysis as the human capacity to influence other people's behavior, even against their will. How can this particular human capacity be related to play as a different capacity, able to deal with two or more ways of classifying reality? The only common characteristic

8. Michael and Chen, *Serious Games.* The authors include religious games in their overview (216–20).

9. Droogers, "Methodological Ludism," 53; Droogers, *Play and Power in Religion,* 321.

10. Pruyser, *Dynamic Psychology of Religion,* 190.

11. Turner, *From Ritual to Theatre,* 25, 169.

appears to be that both are human capacities, but otherwise they represent antithetical intentions and goals. Play depends on making room for more versions. Otherwise there would be little to play with. Alternatives form the raw material that play works with, creating and depicting more realities. Power, however, tends to reduce behavioral alternatives. Its primary interest is to establish a clear, unequivocal, and manageable order. If alternatives are allowed, these are built into the system and correspond with its needs, as in a two-party political system. Rulers tend to maintain their version of reality, frequently viewing alternatives as subversive. That power may lead people to behave in a way that is against their will—defending alternative modes of action—also points to the excluding capacity of those in power. Especially when rulers move from subservient to self-serving power, the contrast with play is reinforced. Subservient power will facilitate free play, without interest, whereas self-serving power will use it for its own purposes.

Power thus reduces possibilities for play, simply by putting limits on the number of alternative views on (aspects of) reality. This strategy can be so successful that people simply are not aware of alternative possibilities. They may even cooperate loyally with the rulers who direct their behavior. Obviously a simple and effective order confers advantages to all involved, not only those who pull the strings. Those subjected to the exercise of power will readily pay the bounty the system imposes in terms of human cost.

As I suggested already, power is useful in making possible a society of thousands, or even millions of meaning-makers. Society is only viable when there is a limit to the possible number of alternatives. Unbridled creativity is not helpful. Wild meaning-making must be curtailed. Societies and states differ in the way they achieve this and in the width of the free margins they permit. Rulers may facilitate access to alternatives, even though "anything goes" is not frequently part of their credo, certainly not when self-serving power is considered normal. Subservient power, however, will leave ample room for alternatives. Though it needs certain conditions to be able to function, these are minimal, other goals being more central. Open societies can thus be distinguished from closed societies, since tolerance is an important value and the climate is non-authoritarian within them.[12]

Interestingly, people who resist particular vestiges of power not only come up with alternatives, but may also use playful methods to make themselves heard. Obviously resistance to some self-serving political systems can be an extremely serious matter, a question of life and death. Violence

12. Popper, *Open Society*.

can be used on both sides. Yet, playfulness and humor can also form part of resistant actions. Even under the most totalitarian regimes, jokes are cracked, and satire forms the undercurrent, causing people to laugh amidst their worries and tears. Protest songs are another expression of alternative views. Each era produces its own Robin Hoods. In some countries, the Web and mobile phones are the most recent modes of acquiring free space. During a recent period of resistance against the Iranian regime, people went to their rooftops after curfew to shout, "Allah is great." The human capacity for meaning-making inspired play with layers of meaning, using covert, conservative language to disguise scathing criticism: "With the help of Allah the regime will find its end."

The contrast between power and play should not be exaggerated. Resistance is, for example, also a way of exercising power. Rulers may make room for playful expressions that go beyond normally acceptable power games, after careful consideration. Such action may provide a visible means of wielding and displaying their own power. Rulers may organize mass events of a sporting or military kind, intended to entertain their subjects. Rulers may also recognize the signs of the times, as Gorbachev did, admitting the need for an alternative society. When a dictatorship is nearing its end, the rulers may use their power to establish a period of transition.

Looking at this from the perspective of play, power is never absent. Play is impossible without a power context that guarantees room to play. Besides, play and power are intermingled in many ways. Children are quick to discover that play involves power differences, and they may be very creative in bending the rules of the game. Sports matches and games usually end with the declaration of a winner. In terms of power, winners are simply superior at influencing their opponent's behavior. Competition is a sufficiently important word for it to be used as a label for a series of games or matches. If teams from different cities or nations play against each other, the game comes to refer to cities or nations, including their power differences. Though only a limited number of players are involved, all fans will say: "We won." The Olympic Games raise not only feelings of global brother/sisterhood, but of exclusive nationalism as well. Leisure activities can also serve as an example. We now speak of a leisure industry with vested interests, including competition and power struggles. The playing human is a source of profit. Games may mirror society. The game Monopoly provides an interesting example of an artificially constructed reality that is very similar to the real world of real estate.

Play and power make a complex couple. They can be distinguished from each other, but often appear to be entangled. If play provides a limitless number of alternatives, power seeks to domesticate wild meaning-making. The result is a compromise about the margins of freedom that are allowed, in custom or written law, or by turning a blind eye to deviations. Changes over time are possible, either amplifying or reducing the number of alternatives. Cities in The Netherlands have "coffee shops," a euphemism for places where soft drugs are sold. The position of these places in law and police practice is a delicate mix of tolerance and censure, made even more fragile because new policies are regularly introduced in reaction to social unrest.

Play and Religion

Looking now at play and religion, the two realities mentioned in the definition of play can be identified as the human and the sacred reality. Thus religion is understood as a form of play. This can be located within the framework sketched in chapter three, and directly connected with the human animal's ability and need for meaning-making set out in chapter two. The human animal's problem is that the capacity for meaning-making serves to control his or her reality, and yet complete control and understanding proves to be impossible. All the sources of religion mentioned in my analysis of the theory of religion are phenomena that escape full signification. In an effort to regain control over these wholes, the human animal plays with the experience of the beyond as an Other, different but approachable. Religions differ in the degree to which this Other is thought to relate to humans. Beliefs vary from those that regard the sacred entity as being absent, or at least far away, to those that regard it as familiar, even incarnated in a human body. In contrast to the possibility of the absent sacred, it can be viewed from the other extreme as being always present, with all reality under its spell. The play with alternative meanings is endless.

With this starting-point, the double reality of religious play, human and sacred, is depicted. The care that has been taken to understand the serious nature of play, applies equally to religious play. The unexpected combination of religion with play can immediately be made plausible by reference to the seriousness that is intrinsic to play. In my understanding of what religion is about, the element of play is crucial, precisely within the parameters that follow from the workings of power. Religion is focused on sacred power, and the concept of power gains additional significance in our treatment of religion. The power dimension, in its human and sacred forms, can moreover be seen as contributing to the seriousness of religious play.

Play in religion not only relates to alternative human and sacred realities, it is also active in giving meaning to all the experiences that believers seek to understand through their religion. In this sense people play with religion, and a plethora of repertoires emerge in this way. In the subjunctive mode previously mentioned, they experiment with the "as is" and the "as if," with suppositions, desires, possibilities, and hypotheses, just as the women did during their vigil around Esteban's corpse. In religions, people tell each other stories that can be true or invented but that answer deeper questions. Even theologians, in their dedication to the truth, have in the course of time experimented with various interpretations and formulations, as theological libraries document.

This process of playful meaning-making includes sacred reality. Though it is the end result that seems to count, as if it exists from eternity to eternity, it is the product of a long meaning-making process with its own dynamics. Even in supposedly traditional or conservative religions, this process goes on, its influence depending on the margin left open by power. Once given names, symbols, meanings, and significance, just as the women did for Esteban, the sacred is opened to communication. As we saw, the secular power structure and its forms of communication provide a model for exchanges with the sacred powers that be. The religion's power structure will determine the degrees of access to the sacred that are available to different categories of believers. Self-serving types of power will have dissimilar forms of communication with the sacred, compared with subservient forms. In the first type, the divine may be as inaccessible as secular rulers are, in the latter, the sacred can be part of the family, a friend of the house, as ancestor spirits are in many tribal traditional religions, approached in kinship terms. Interestingly, in those cases the Supreme God is often depicted as absent, as unimportant, as having found a reason to withdraw from the earth. Mysticism occurs in various religions, with believers drawing close to the sacred, the institution usually condemning such a transgression of established boundaries. Mysticism can therefore be interpreted as a critique of distance with regard to the sacred that self-serving power imposed, projecting its own view on power to the relationship with the divine. There is often a tense relationship between mystics and religious leadership.

In seeking answers to the ontological, ethical, epistemological, aesthetic, and identity questions (see the Introduction), playful meaning-making results in a huge variation of beliefs and practices. Living and dead, good and evil, true and false, beauty and ugliness, balance and imbalance, and other pairs, may enter the repertoires that religions develop, maintain, and alter. The repertoires of the five world religions, including those of their different factions, together prove the extensions of human meaning-making. If we add to this the repertoires of the thousands of tribal religions, plus those of the new religions that have emerged in the last century, the score of human meaning-making is impressive. Both balanced and one-sided views are possible. Just as open societies can be distinguished from closed societies, there can be open and closed religions. Power interests may influence the choices made. They may also invite resistance and revival, alternatives may be uncovered, or salvaged from oblivion and in spite of censorship. There may be a tidal movement between extreme positions washing through all that lies between them. New developments create new questions. Orthodox Jews, after the introduction of the new fashion, the divided skirt, had to decide whether this was a skirt (appropriate for women), or pants (appropriate for men, not women). To give another example: deism provided a nice solution once science began to change the worldview. The innovation was to depict the Creator as a watch maker, admitting the idea that after winding up the watch, he simply left it alone, nature following its own course, open to scientific research about the laws of the mechanism.

In our times, with modernization and subsequent individualization, the process of meaning-making is no longer controlled by the institution to the same degree as it once was. As a consequence, individual persons compose their own package of ideas and practices. They no longer respect the boundaries that religious leadership used to maintain. Elements from different religions are freely selected and combined, in a consistent way or with a number of contradictions. Secular elements may be part of the personal package. Playful meaning-making receives a boost from these trends. The religious variety that already existed is extended, with many individual innovations along the way. At the same time, and in reaction, bordering religions protect their identity and control the meaning-making of their believers.

Two Hemispheres

As we saw, over the last decades cognitive studies set the trend in theorizing religion. Findings about how the brain functions are considered in light of what we know about religion. There is a tendency to reduce religion to the human mind's material conditions, but there are also less reductionist efforts, detecting possible links between religion and the human brain. Though the results of brain research are sometimes presented as the ultimate answer, there is a variety of approaches, and moreover more "second thoughts" than "no-brainers" ("mind" the pun!). In fact, the way students of religion use the varied and provisional results from cognitive studies can be viewed as an example of academic meaning-making, selecting some meanings as relevant and relegating other insights as useless. In my view, the cognitive approach, though fashionable, is not without value, at least when I take the opportunity to make my own selection from meanings and insights. I do not take the outcome of cognitive studies as my starting-point, unlike other scholars. My interest is triggered by the impression that some results appear to support the type of approach to religion that I am developing in this book.

What is it in the cognitive approach that most closely corresponds with the perspective on religion developed so far? Is there a cognitive perspective on the human animal's wild but domesticated meaning-making? What would such an approach say about the human effort to make sense of experiences that are beyond understanding and control, including meaning-making itself?

Cognitive studies have something to tell about human meaning-making, including its playful side. They explore the possibilities that the oversized brain puts at the disposition of the human meaning-making animal. My guide in the cognitive field is psychiatrist Iain McGilchrist's recent study *The Master and His Emissary*.[13] The attraction for me in his work resides in the conscious effort to link what happens in the brain with what occurs in Western culture, especially through modernization. Moreover his approach seeks to clarify what happens during the process of meaning-making. In addition to this, I draw from the connectionist approach in cognitive anthropology.[14] In this section I summarize their cognitive insights,

13. McGilchrist, *The Master and His Emissary*.

14. D'Andrade, *Development of Cognitive Anthropology*, 122–49; Bloch, "Language, Anthropology and Cognitive Science"; Strauss and Quinn, *Cognitive Theory*, 48–88.

applying them in the next section to my appraisal of religion, power, and play.

The physical outfit of the human animal prepares him (or her) for his role as a meaning-maker. The evolutionary jump in the growth of the brain is primarily related to the frontal lobes, which are instrumental in the human ability "to stand back from the world, from ourselves, and from the immediacy of experience. . . . If it has made us the most powerful and destructive of animals, it has also turned us, famously, into the 'social animal,' and into an animal with a spiritual dimension."[15]

What then are the respective properties of the two hemispheres that are crucial to the human animal's performance? Though the hemispheres share some characteristics, each has its own abilities, complementary with those of the other. "It is a system of opponent processors," McGilchrist has argued.[16] The left hemisphere maps and makes standard what the right hemisphere explores in an open way. In McGilchrist's assessment:

> the left hemisphere tends to deal more with pieces of information in isolation, and the right hemisphere with the entity as a whole, the so-called Gestalt—possibly underlying and helping to explain the apparent verbal/visual dichotomy, since words are processed serially, while pictures are taken in all at once.[17]

The hemispheres differ, the vigilant right being characterized by connotation and ongoing association, the designing left by denotation and static unequivocalness. The right hemisphere is the domain of mutual connections between patterns, contexts, words, metaphors, and meanings. It also controls social relations, viewing the self in connection with other selves. It is the hemisphere where poetry, art, faces, humor, irony, and the implicit are easily recognized and processed. All these phenomena are not directly recognizable to the left half, yet they are open to its dissecting gaze. The purpose-directed left hemisphere deals more easily and in an explicit way with single parts, neat distinctions, unambiguous signs, abstract prose, the isolated self as one unit, the various elements that compose the face. It does not recognize the wink and tends to explain a joke, irony, a painting, or metaphor.[18] It does away with ambiguity. The left half enjoys its results.

15. McGilchrist, *The Master and His Emissary*, 21, 22.
16. Ibid., 9.
17. Ibid., 4.
18. Ibid., 182.

It naturally reifies its findings, presenting them as the real, the final result of brain activity.[19]

The bi-hemispheric structure of the brain is fundamental to the way we look at our world and even construct our image of it, basically combining the perspectives of individuation and coherence.[20] The contrast between left and right encompasses earlier and familiar distinctions such as those drawn between Apollo and Dionysus in Greek mythology,[21] the indicative "as is" and the subjunctive "as if" mentioned earlier when discussing the definition of play, and the hedgehog and the fox in Isaiah Berlin's version of the opposition.[22] It represents two ways of life. In the end, the specificity of each hemisphere does not stem from what it manages—language, emotion, reason, religion—nor from its concrete functions, but from the way in which it handles input.[23] A specific type of relationship is an intrinsic characteristic of each hemisphere, the right half starting with aggregates, the left taking parts as more important.[24] Accordingly, we get very different versions whether we use both halves simultaneously or prioritize one half. The effect is even stronger since each version not only *describes*, but also tends to *prescribe* our perspective.[25] We don't know better than what the hemisphere's versions make available to us.

The broad distinction between the hemispheres determines the way information is processed. Unique, personal, empathic, bodily, and emotionally perceived knowledge results from personal involvement via the right hemisphere, whereas generic, abstract, impersonal knowledge is the version derived from the detached position that the left half occupies. The right hemisphere is of crucial importance in exploring and mediating new experience and information.[26] In the left hemisphere, those pre-reflective experiences from the right half are re-presented, and processed into a

19. Ibid., 181.

20. Ibid., 203.

21. Ibid., 199, 284, 382.

22. The fox knows many things, but the hedgehog knows one big thing, according to the Greek poet Archilochus (680–645 B.C.). Isaiah Berlin wrote of Tolstoy that he was a fox who wished he were a hedgehog. Berlin, *The Hedgehog and the Fox.*

23. McGilchrist *The Master and His Emissary*, 29, 64, 70, 93.

24. Ibid., 54.

25. Ibid., 4, 5.

26. Ibid., 27.

focused, localized, everyday, and selective version, different because it contains

> static, separable, bounded, but essentially fragmented entities, grouped in classes, on which predictions can be based. . . . [I]t renders things inert, mechanical, lifeless. But it also enables us for the first time to know, and consequently to learn and to make things. This gives us power.[27]

In processing information, the vigilant right half, the open "mind," registers the new before it is submitted to the routine analysis that is the left half's specialty, working with what it knows already; as a consequence the right hemisphere is "more capable of a frame shift,"[28] more flexibly admitting alternatives.

> [T]he left hemisphere needs certainty and needs to be right. The right hemisphere makes it possible to hold several ambiguous possibilities in suspension together without premature closure on one outcome. . . . The right hemisphere's tolerance of uncertainty is implied everywhere in its subtle ability to use metaphors, irony and humour, all of which depend on not prematurely resolving ambiguities. So, of course, does poetry, which relies on right-hemisphere language capacities.[29]

The right hemisphere has the master role, putting the left half as its emissary to work and expecting to get its feedback of processed experience, to then reach a synthesis.[30] The basic principle is that "the rational workings of the left hemisphere . . . should be subject to the intuitive wisdom of the right hemisphere."[31] The right half has primacy over the left because affect, unconsciousness, and experience have precedence over ratio, consciousness, and cognitive abstraction.[32] As McGilchrist puts it, employing a metaphor that is more right than left-hemispheric, "Reality has a roundness rather than rectilinearity."[33]

---

27. Ibid., 31.
28. Ibid., 40.
29. Ibid., 82, cf. 229.
30. Ibid., 46, 176–208.
31. Ibid., 203.
32. Ibid., 186–89.
33. Ibid., 177.

He suggests that the developments in modernizing Western culture stimulate left hemisphere functions more than those from the right, thereby shifting the balance of power between the two halves.[34] Following from the Enlightenment and the rise of science, and despite the Renaissance's penchant for "standing-back,"[35] Western culture appeals much more to the left than to the right hemisphere. "The model of the machine is the only one that the left hemisphere likes,"[36] suggests the left hemisphere's affinity with modernization and industrialization, which in turn create "a world in the left hemisphere's own likeness."[37] In the Western world we are recently "busy imitating machines."[38] The sorcerer's apprentice has an overactive left hemisphere, losing sight of the whole of her or his actions. The left hemisphere is also the domain of the cult of the hungry dragon that I depicted in chapter two as being typical of our era.

The right hemisphere, focused on the whole, is in the first instance able to take in the panoramic perspective and is therefore, in McGilchrist's view, "the Master" and the left hemisphere "the Emissary." However, these roles are not fixed and the emissary now tends to behave more and more like the new master. The emissary becomes busy preparing a putsch, the two hemispheres become involved in a power struggle.[39] Power is the prime motivation of the left hemisphere.[40] Moreover, "the left hemisphere is better able to suppress the right than the right is able to suppress the left."[41] Of the left hemisphere it can be said that "[m]anipulation and use require clarity and fixity, and clarity and fixity require separation and division. . . . It is the hemisphere of 'either/or': clarity yields sharp boundaries. And so it makes divisions that may not exist according to the right hemisphere."[42]

Using a topical metaphor, McGilchrist suggests that the left hemisphere "is like the Berlusconi of the brain, a political heavyweight who has control of the media."[43] Viewed from the left hemisphere, with its

34. Ibid., 6, 7, 158, 252. The second half of his book is dedicated to this thesis.
35. Ibid., 298 cf. 328.
36. Ibid., 98.
37. Ibid., 386.
38. Ibid., 256.
39. Ibid., 204.
40. Ibid., 209.
41. Ibid., 46, 218.
42. Ibid., 137.
43. Ibid., 229.

emphasis on exact knowledge, the right hemisphere, allowing degrees of not-knowing, has the weaker position.[44] "The left hemisphere is not impressed by empathy: its concern is with maximising gain for itself, and its driving value is utility."[45] Viewed by the left, the right may even be seen as a tyrant, the enemy of its exclusive mechanistic perspective.[46] However, "the business of living calls forth aspects of things in either hemisphere."[47] The choice is between

> an essentially divisive drive to acquisition, power and manipulation, based on competition, which sets individual against individual, in the service of unitary survival; and an essentially cohesive drive towards cooperation, synergy and mutual benefit, based on collaboration, in the service of the survival of the group.[48]

Or as Miguel de Unamuno succinctly put it in 1912, without knowing about brain hemispheres:

> [L]iving is one thing and knowing is another, and . . . perhaps there is such an opposition between the two that we may say that everything vital is anti-rational, not merely irrational, and that everything rational is anti-vital. And this is the basis of the tragic sense of life.[49]

Whereas in the course of human history the way in which the hemispheres relate has changed with the cultural context, in McGilchrist's view tension is increasing nowadays in an unprecedented way. This contaminates our way of looking at ourselves.

> An increasingly mechanistic, fragmented, decontextualised world, marked by unwarranted optimism mixed with paranoia and a feeling of emptiness, has come about, reflecting, I believe, the unopposed action of a dysfunctional left hemisphere. . . . It behooves us to be skeptical.[50]

---

44. Ibid., 175.
45. Ibid., 145.
46. Ibid., 206.
47. Ibid., 154.
48. Ibid., 128.
49. Unamo, *Tragic Sense of Life*, 18.
50. McGilchrist, *The Master and His Emissary*, 6.

The disciplines that specialize on our self-image do not escape this trend. To the contrary, most modern philosophers examine "the life of the right hemisphere from the standpoint of the left."[51]

> [T]he default approach of philosophy is that of the left hemisphere, since it is via denotative language and linear, sequential analysis that we pin things down and make them clear and precise, and pinning them down and making them clear and precise equates with seeing the truth, as far as the left hemisphere is concerned.[52]

This is a reversal of what has long been the norm. "I believe that, despite appearances, philosophy begins and ends in the right hemisphere, though it has to journey through the left hemisphere on its way."[53] Even neuroscience does not escape left-hemisphere manipulation, since it emphasizes more the *what* than *in what way*, being blind to the contributions made by the right hemisphere, which is often depicted as silent and minor.[54] Intellectuals can be said to be "lefties" by profession!

To McGilchrist's grim view of our current predicament, I now add some elements taken from the connectionist approach, especially the role of what I call schema repertoires.[55] A schema can be defined as *a culturally accepted minimal script (or scenario, prototype, frame, or model) for and of a certain act, thought, emotion, or perception.*[56] Schemas are representational, but also serve as processors. They contain a limited number of elements, which are common to similar concrete situations, for example, a visit to a restaurant or to a GP. Claudia Strauss and Naomi Quinn define schemas as "networks of strongly connected cognitive elements that represent the generic concepts stored in memory."[57] The generic quality and the minimal format prepare them for application in a variety of situations. They are like an empty bureaucratic form that can be filled out differently in each concrete case. Human beings, including scholars, constantly use schemas to make sense of the field they happen to be active in. They constantly play

51. Ibid., 89.

52. Ibid., 135.

53. Ibid., 156.

54. Ibid., 93, 129.

55. Parts of what is included here were published previously, Droogers, *Play and Power in Religion*, 118–23.

56. Cf. D'Andrade, *Development of Cognitive Anthropology*, 122.

57. Strauss and Quinn, *Cognitive Theory of Cultural Meaning*, 6.

with alternative schemas, just as I do in this book, proposing or altering other schemas.

Schemas are physically anchored in the brain as connections (therefore connectionism) between millions of neurons and generate corporeal experiences, just as experiences inspire the formation or alteration of schemas. In terms of the hemispheres, the right half comes with an experience that the left hemisphere makes a generic schema of and for, feeding it back to the right hemisphere that, as the director of the human movie, has the overview over the whole set, making registration and subsequent performance possible.

Schemas do not stand alone. Simpler schemas can be embedded in more complex schemas.[58] In case of complicated applications, schemas may have subschemas and sub-sub-schemas, as is the case in relation to legislation, jurisprudence continuously adding new variants. To characterize a set of schemas, I use the metaphor of the repertoire. Just like musicians' or actors' repertoires, schema repertoires are open to changes, yet are the durable mainstay of a concrete performance in a particular field. The schemas in a repertoire are only partially used, rarely as a whole. Since they apply to different concrete contexts, they may contain contradictions and inconsistencies. They are socially built and controlled.

Cultures and religions contain many schema repertoires, each organized in a particular way, for example, hierarchically, causally, or like the branches on a tree. Some fields have very specialized repertoires, only known to and used by specialists in that field, for example some schema repertoires in religion, such as ritual or theology. Modern science abounds with special repertoires for ever smaller branches of the academic tree. They show continuity, but may also obey the commandment of constant innovation, although the new finding may imply only a minor shuffle of neurons in the schemas.

Schemas as well as repertoires differ in their durability, their flexibility, and their resistance to new influences. They can become rigid and formal, just as they set the stage for exploration and improvisation. Traditions belong to the fixed category, conscious innovation to the second. The tenacity of the schemas and repertoires is reflected in the more or less permanent connections between billions of neurons.[59] Socialization is a process that establishes and conditions these more or less permanent connections in

58. D'Andrade, *Development of Cognitive Anthropology*, 124.
59. Strauss and Quinn, *Cognitive Theory of Cultural Meaning*, 51.

the brain. Education is a form of brain washing. Fixed connections are essential for predictable routine behavior. Rebels resist established traditional patterns.

When confronted with a new situation, the brain rapidly selects or produces the schema that best fits the as-yet-not-interpreted situation, alternating between induction and deduction. This process is in fact a simultaneous consultation in the right hemisphere of a number of repertoires, with even more schemas. Once a selection is made, the language repertoire is consulted in similar ways. Finally (i.e., after milliseconds), the conclusion is verbalized, which is the task of the left hemisphere. That spoken or written conclusion appears to deny the preceding inchoate parallel simultaneity, suggesting the fiction of a clear, linear way of proceeding. Education usually relies on such linear statements, as do you and I, as reader and author of this book. Our activities however include incessant experiential exercises that stem from the processes of parallel schema consultation in the right hemisphere. As a reader, you have to recognize the words as patterns of lines with a meaning. As the author, I trust that we are both thinking of the same meaning. Our brains have to work hard to reach that point, the right hemisphere simultaneously consulting many repertoire archives, feeding the left hemisphere with tasks that may involve experimenting with new schemas.[60]

Straightforward language will function in this routine manner. Irony and double meaning, however, demand extra effort, appealing more to parallel rather than linear thinking. And so does creativity. Similarly, one must keep "in mind" that a description of a culture's or a religion's customs is far removed from the people's connectionist experience with the rapid alternation of induction and deduction—which they themselves are mostly unaware of. Below the cultural or religious static surface, many layers of meaning-processing show a constant dynamic activity, sometimes causing earthquakes in meaning-making. Modern culture is characterized by a huge stimulation of these processes. The connections in the schema repertoires in the modern human animal's oversized brain show the presence of constant heavy traffic. Globalization is adding to the repertoires at an unprecedented speed, giving the human animal an ever expanding archive of repertoires that are also subject to rapid change. Although one might expect a homogeneous world culture to emerge, in fact diversity is stronger

---

60. D'Andrade, *Development of Cognitive Anthropology*, 139–41.

than ever, because of the free mixing of elements from many sources, producing new combinations.

The Hemispheres and Religion

This very selective reading of the cognitive approach helps me to rethink in turn my version of the human animal's religion, including the role attributed to power and play. Religion then appears as a special illustration in which power and play, represented by the left and the right hemisphere respectively, are in constant tension. As McGilchrist puts it:

> [I]f the process ends with the left hemisphere, one has only concepts—abstractions and conceptions. . . . [T]he immediate preconceptual sense of awe can evolve into religion only with the help of the left hemisphere: though, if the process stops there, all one has is theology, or sociology, or empty ritual: something else.[61]

Left-hemisphere activity is indispensable, but includes a strong risk. The tragic fate of the human animal stems in large part from this inbuilt tension. The beautiful tool-kit of the meaning-maker may easily spin out of control. Religion, especially in its bordering forms, constantly illustrates the risk that the left hemisphere represents. What McGilchrist views as a consequence of Enlightenment thinking, has in my view been present in religion for as long as it has existed. In religion, the emissary has all the opportunities to dethrone the master.

The human animal's need to control his endless meaning-making is well served by the left hemisphere and its uses of power, which I defined earlier as the human capacity to influence other people's behavior, even against their will. Alternatives are efficiently limited to a functional number. Endless meaning-making is kept active by the right hemisphere, play—defined earlier as the human capacity to deal simultaneously and subjunctively with two or more ways of classifying reality—corresponding with, and made possible by the constant and simultaneous comparison of repertoires and schemas. The two hemispheres serve not only as a metaphor for the inner struggle that is characteristic of the human animal, they are the physical cause of that tension. Power and play complement each other as long as the left and right hemispheres are in equilibrium. The cycle from experience, to reflection, to integration in the whole, is then guaranteed,

---

61. McGilchrist, *The Master and His Emissary*, 199.

both hemispheres having their own role in the processing of old and new schemas. Thus play can contribute without degenerating into endless meaning-making, power serving to create some form of order without silencing the right hemisphere.

Yet, as we saw already when discussing the influence of power, the balance is precarious. Distortion is likely. The process that McGilchrist describes in relation to modern Western culture appears to have been normal practice in religions from the start. Very soon after the religious virtuoso had his founding experience and spread the word, the creative imagination that the right hemisphere facilitated, was curbed by the left hemisphere. Power is inevitable and useful, but very early into the history of a religious movement, and especially in the phase of developing strong institutions, it becomes self-serving. Only where subservient power prevailed, in sectors where the officials of the institution had no control, as in popular religion, could the right hemisphere continue to play its role, keeping access to alternatives open. Basically it seems that religious leaders fear the wild thinking that is part of the human animal's peculiar condition, because they are afraid of the role it will play in messing with the experiential base of their power position. The inchoate nature of alternative religious experience seems dangerous to them. From their perspective the alternative experience cries out to be pruned back. In the end religious leaders can be too radical, eradicating root and branch at once.

The picture that thus emerges is that of the tragic human animal, at constant war with himself (or herself), both in the hemispheres of the brain and in real life, being fascinated by the immense possibilities of his thinking and yet constantly restrained by power structures. Wild untamed reflection needs to be controlled, but it is then reduced to the status of a lion in a tiny cage. It is allowed to roar now and then, but cannot roam freely and thus restlessly walks the same ground over and over. Religion, though potentially and from its origins imaginative, has turned out to be one of the lion's most fanatical guards. The roaring at the start of a movement soon turns into the phase of standardized doctrine and ritual, about which only the specialists know the deeper meaning.

As we saw earlier, the self-conscious human animal simultaneously stands apart from the surrounding reality, observing it, and yet wishes to be part of his reality and take part in it, being sensitive to the occurrence of transcending wholes.[62] The abilities of self-reflection and distinction,

62. Baal, *Symbols for Communication*, 219 ff.; cf. McGilchrist, *The Master and His*

mentioned in McGilchrist's model, resulted in the immense variation in cultures and religions and in their continuous amendment, albeit only when the power structure leaves room to do so, usually in an institution-alized manner. Although all humans work with roughly the same brain structure, its universal ability is to make diversity possible. Accordingly, the variety of signification is carried to excess, even within one culture or religion, widely beyond the minimum that is functionally necessary. Thus the accumulated schema repertoires of all religions taken together testify to the unlimited imagination of the right hemisphere, whereas the high walls surrounding and between the same religions express the degree of control as well as the bordered tendencies that the left hemisphere imposes, with its focus on utility and power. The creative view on the whole is replaced by a fragmented, mechanistic perspective.

What I am looking to do in writing this book, is to make an argument for the rehabilitation within religion of the playful activity and thus of the right hemisphere, against the dominion of the powerful left hemisphere. This amounts to a recovery of the aggregate view, which is central to the ex-planation of religion I provided in chapter three. Since power is inevitable, just as the left hemisphere is necessary, my distinction between subservi-ent and self-serving power should help to open a context for exploring the margins, looking for the room that is left open to play, offering alternative perspectives on the experience of wholes. This includes retaining some control over the unlimited tendencies of play. My definition of play speaks of "two or more ways of classifying reality," suggesting a limitation already.

What I suggested about the start of religious movements may serve as an example of what, in principle, is possible. Yet, McGilchrist's character-ization of the left hemisphere, as manipulative and self-serving, is not en-couraging. In religion, the emissary has, for as long as religion has existed, already played the role of the master. The chance that the right hemisphere and its playful role can be rehabilitated demands a strong faith.

The picture is no more positive if we look at concrete religious phe-nomena and their link with the two hemispheres and their power struggle. Many schemas appear to serve the interests of those in power, especially those of the self-serving type. The schema repertoires that belong to doc-trine, ritual, vocabulary, and hierarchy in religions with an outspoken power structure, illustrate this. Theologians of any religion appear to be-have like the philosophers and neuroscientists that McGilchrist criticized,

---

Emissary, 85, 87, 128, 140, 202, 320.

looking at the right hemisphere from the perspective of the left hemisphere, thereby confirming the distorted religious power constellation. Though some theologians explore the frontiers and the margins, others legitimate the stasis that the left hemisphere is familiar with. The religion's source will fall dry accordingly, for lack of insights into the dynamics of wholes in human experience. The cyclical movement from right hemisphere, to left and back again is cut short, making the left hemisphere and its mechanistic utility thinking the victor.

This is also often the way of religious movements, as we saw when we discussed their cycle. Ecstatic behavior, typical at the first stage of a movement, is soon rendered harmless, the left hemisphere doing its job efficiently, domesticating what comes from the right. Sooner or later mechanistic forms of faith predominate.[63]

Though conservative and fundamentalist religions appear to be the most bordered, the phenomenon is not limited to that sector of religious activity. The tendency to put an end to ambiguities, inconsistencies, and paradoxes is strong. The tentative search for answers to the basic questions of life is halted as soon as the results of the quest are promoted to the realm of exclusive truth. The subjunctive "as if" is marginalized by the indicative "as is." "Language, it would seem, starts out with what looks like imperial aspirations."[64] Once put into words, the experience is no longer fresh, and the word does not always succeed in evoking the event.

If McGilchrist's grim predictions have always been the reality in religions, and the prospects for playful religion thus seem limited, some consolation may be gained from the idea that in the course of time the relation between the two hemispheres can change. The transitions between, for example, the Renaissance and the Enlightenment, and from there to Romanticism, have been rather seamless.[65] If the left hemisphere is in the front row, doing all the talking, this does not exclude a significant role for the right, even when it seems to have been silenced in its subordinate position. The awareness of the influence that the two hemispheres have on our versions of reality and thus on our behavior, may help us to reflect on the possibility of inverting the prevailing bordering state of religious affairs.

63. For an interesting example, see Johannesen, "Third-Generation Pentecostal Language."

64. McGilchrist, *The Master and His Emissary*, 114.

65. Ibid., 352.

Here, in taking sides, in moving away from the position of an observing scholar, I become a participant.

The approach proposed in chapter three, when I sought to explain religion, may offer a lead. The role of wholes that escape human control and understanding was emphasized. Interestingly wholes are the right hemisphere's specialty, as are images, allowing for the expression of what cannot be said in words. What overwhelms us is experienced as an uncontrollable totality, the right hemisphere's domain. These wholes can be viewed as the religion's main sources. Their inclusion in the explanation of religion is a way of returning the right hemisphere to its potential position of mastery. To me it is not simply a matter of objective explanation, but of subjective re-integration. Give me that old-time religion. Wild reflection was presented as the main source, being the most basic whole, and in fact, when described in terms of the right hemisphere's qualifications, we can identify its workshop in the human oversized brain. We now can also understand what is needed to tame its abundance without killing it off. The condition is the feedback from left hemisphere to the right. This may include a return from proportion and system to inchoate experience. Visions and images can play a role again, recovered from iconoclastic fury. The word can become flesh again, after the flesh was reduced to the word, as McGilchrist puts it.[66]

McGilchrist makes this observation in relation to a discussion about the Reformation.[67] Since it shows the difficulties religions have in managing the two hemispheres in a balanced way, it is worthwhile summarizing his analysis. The Reformation, in its critique of rituals in their degenerated, inauthentic, and corrupt mediaeval form, did not lead to a renewed metaphoric understanding, but to an outright rejection of all images. Even though Luther rehabilitated authentic experience, this did not prevent iconoclastic fury from occurring. The potential of the right hemisphere in stimulating imagination was thus ignored. In good lefty style, the visual image, one of the right half's vehicles, was taken literally—the image is the saint—and therefore abandoned. In reaction, the word—the left hemisphere's domain—was given a central place, the pulpit replacing the altar. Thus the left hemisphere, with its either/or approach, had the opportunity to dictate the Reformation's agenda. Consequently the "Reformation is the first great expression for certainty in modern times."[68] It resisted the

66. Ibid., 323.
67. Ibid., 314–23.
68. Ibid., 315.

Renaissance's balancing efforts and perfectly matched Enlightenment perspectives that saw metaphor at best as mere adornment, decoration to be mistrusted.[69] The choices made in the Reformation also had consequences for perspectives on power.[70] McGilchrist offers a profile of Reformation power that has more general relevance:

> The power-hungry will always aim to substitute explicit for intuitive understanding. Intuitive understanding is not under control, and therefore cannot be trusted by those who wish to manipulate and dominate the way we think; for them it is vital that such contexts, with their hidden powerful meanings that have accrued through sometimes millennia of experience, are eradicated.[71]

Surprisingly, a movement that potentially could have helped to restore the balance between the two hemispheres, sided with the left hemisphere, thereby adopting bordering characteristics. The Reformation is an example of the rapidity with which a religious movement can deviate from an original intention.

Yet, the idea that history could have taken a different course gives reason for some optimism. Awareness of the wrong turns taken in these processes can help us to find better ways to deal with the brain of the human animal. In this way, we may rediscover old schemas and repertoires, and invent new ones. The urgency of the problems of our era may convince us of the need to end the dictatorship of the left hemisphere.

Reconsiderations

There are three observations I would still like to make with regard to the cognitive aspect and the study of religion, and in so doing, shed new light on earlier debates. The first concerns the distinction often made between religion and magic, the second the functionalist approach, and the third Girard's theory mentioned in the previous chapter. In all three cases the schemas used reveal how they correspond to the labor division between the two hemispheres.

69. Ibid., 318, 337.
70. Ibid., 321, 322.
71. Ibid., 319.

The concepts of religion and magic refer to an old debate in the study of religion.[72] Though magic can be seen as part of religion, the two also contrast significantly. Interestingly, the characteristics once attributed to religion and magic mirror the properties of the right and left hemispheres respectively. The selection of these characteristics is influenced by one specific schema repertoire, influenced by the Christian distinction between true and false religion. Admittedly, my plea for a playful religion and against self-serving power is a variation on this theme, but an inversion, putting powerful religion on the false side, perhaps much to the surprise of self-serving leadership. Usually the self-serving powers in religion have used the labels "magic" and "false" for any religious expression that they considered to be heretical. Besides, the passive submission to divine power was considered religious, and its active manipulation magical, corresponding to the right hemisphere's experience of wholes versus the left hemisphere's focus on utility. This could be a first step for the conversion of self-serving leadership. Religion has also been depicted as social, whereas magic was seen as individual or even anti-social, thereby obeying some of the characteristics that McGilchrist mentioned: either individual against individual, or cohesive synergy. Magic has also been interpreted as based on an error, taking metaphors literally, thus more leftish than rightish. The cognitive perspective presented here relocates the debate on religion and magic into a new context. From the playful perspective, and taking manipulation and utility as magic's core traits, the term magic would apply primarily to the self-serving type of religion and power, anchored as it is in the left hemisphere.

The second debate relates to the functionalist approach. It can also be reinterpreted in terms of the two brain hemispheres. It looks at religion from the perspective of the mechanistic cause-and-effect reasoning that is typically at home in the left side of the brain.[73] As we saw in chapter three, functionalist explanations have some shortcomings, which can now be identified as the consequence of the functionalist preference for the left hemisphere. Neglecting or ignoring the right hemisphere's role and quality, the utilitarian scope is too narrow. Because of its utilitarian focus on order and its conditions, functionalist theory corresponds with a leaders' way of

---

72. Lehmann and Myers, *Magic, Witchcraft, and Religion.*

73. Rational choice theories of religion also appear to be exclusively focused on the left hemisphere's abilities. Cognitive theories of religion may suffer the same shortcoming if the left-oriented gaze prevails.

thinking, which makes it attractive in terms of policy advice. The functionalist theories do not explain differences between religions, since all of them are supposed to have the same functions. Nor do they clarify the abundant use of symbolism, beyond functional necessity. In other words, they are not specific enough since to them, the use of religion is the main question. The mechanistic perspective even allows for the inclusion of ideologies, even anti-religious ones with similar functions. And then there was the article of faith that a religion's functions were there from the start, even though not embraced by the founder and only attributed retrospectively by the modern student of religion. The theory I presented in that same chapter cannot ignore the functional gaze of the left hemisphere. In fact, it gave it a place. However, in pointing to the role of wholes, the right hemisphere was given a crucial role in the appreciation of religion.

Girard explains religion from the perspective of the need to control mimetic desire. The stages progressing from envy, through the scapegoat mechanism, to regained harmony, correspond with the human brain structure. McGilchrist, in characterizing the behavior that the two hemispheres stimulate, draws this distinction between them:

> an essentially divisive drive to acquisition, power and manipulation, based on competition, which sets individual against individual, in the service of unitary survival; and an essentially cohesive drive towards cooperation, synergy and mutual benefit, based on collaboration, in the service of the survival of the group.[74]

The mimetic desire, even when taken as a modern myth, illustrates the contrast. Whereas the envy that is the result of the individual's imitating desire threatens to destroy the social texture, pitting individual against individual, the survival of the group is served, in Girard's view, by the scapegoat mechanism, leading to a religion that renews peace and harmony. This perspective on religion appears to move from left to right hemisphere, from the self-serving type of power to the subservient kind that is rooted in the right brain. The turn is metaphorically expressed by the rehabilitation of the scapegoat, first sacrificed, then sacralized.

---

74. McGilchrist, *The Master and His Emissary*, 128.

Conclusion

Now that play has been introduced and defined, its connections with several themes that are central to the argument of this book could be discussed. In this inventory, the ramifications of play were shown, first of all by demonstrating how it corresponds with the characteristics of the human animal. The relationship with power was analyzed, in view of both contrasts and complementarities. The tension between the two was recognized to engender wide-ranging repercussions. Play was also shown to be useful as a concept in our understanding of religion, though hidden and with most people being unaware of its role as a human ability. The potential as well as the limits of the role of play were highlighted. The term was then brought into the limelight of a particular cognitive approach, which confirmed a number of insights. McGilchrist's ideas proved to be useful in deepening our understanding of the relationship between religions, power, and play. His appraisal of the scary potential of the left hemisphere in modern times was extended into the context of religion and religions.

Bordering phenomena, as we saw from the start, come in a number of shades and variations. It can be understood as a way of controlling the impact of the playful, and sometimes wild and ecstatic meaning-makers. In establishing boundaries, the frontier mentality of the playful believer is lost. So too are the potential contributions conferred by the right hemisphere, because the bordering process leans heavily on the abilities of the left hemisphere. This offers security, order, and utility. It seems that bordering is exaggerating in its efforts to manage the playful believer. Depending on the strength of the bordering trend, this means that bordering religions contribute to the general tendency to give priority to the left hemisphere's functions in the modern world. As we saw, weighty questions are thereby ignored. In the next chapter, we will examine their relevance and the urgent need for solutions.

Nurse's Song

When voices of children are heard on the green
And laughing is heard on the hill,
My heart is at rest within my breast
And everything else is still.

"Then come home, my children, the sun is gone down
And the dews of night arise;
Come, come, leave off play, and let us away
Till the morning appears in the skies."

"No, no, let us play, for it is yet day
And we cannot go to sleep;
Besides, in the sky, the little birds fly
And the hills are all cover'd with sheep."

"Well, well, go & play till the light fades away
And then go home to bed."
The little ones leaped & shouted & laugh'd
And all the hills ecchoed.

— *William Blake*

six

Weighty Questions Reconsidered

Introduction

AT THE START OF this book, when introducing the bordering phenomenon, I mentioned a number of weighty questions that bordering believers often ignore, although these questions are part of public discourse and may possess a certain kind of urgency. The bordering phenomenon could be defined by taking the negation of these questions as a defining characteristic. The four questions related to *religious diversity, the God debate, the role of power*, and finally *the global problems* (of poverty, violence, pollution, and conflict). In chapter five, playful religion was presented as a type of religiosity that is closer to the origins of religion in general and of concrete religions in particular. In seeking a way of dealing with bordering tendencies, the playful type of religion may play a major role. To test this affirmation, in this final chapter I will discuss each of the weighty questions, suggesting how they can be dealt with in a way that helps humanity in its survival, reducing the human cost involved. The playful approach invites us to look at these questions in a different way and thereby also to reconsider the bordering process. Moreover, in this way we can explore the conditions under which the sustainability of religion can be ensured. The role that religion/religions may play in the twenty-first century can thus be explored. This analysis has consequences for religious educators as well as for those whose trade is the study of religion.

Religious Diversity

Globalization has made religious diversity visible. The accessibility of mass media also means that knowledge about other religions is widely available. The study of religion has been developing since the nineteenth century, greatly contributing to public awareness of other religions. Via the media this knowledge has been popularized. Religious elements play a role in news stories, most of all since terrorism is a global problem, but also in other respects, such as on the occasion of Papal visits. The Arab Spring has drawn our attention to the role of Islam, both in its progressive and more conservative forms. Religious diversity, in its glaringly obvious forms, cannot escape our attention.

An anticipated outcome of religious diversity is that variety in religion would become an issue. The question could arise as to what can be considered true if each religion claims to have the only valid worldview. That religions have to find a way to share the world, is another theme that emerges from this. How can religions contribute to a healthy world society if they consider all other religions false? If we take into account that religions differ in their views on the ideal society and come with incompatible blueprints, then the role of religions in global society is not without complications. There is some work to be done.

Though these questions may seem obvious, it is part of the bordering tendency to ignore them. As we saw, these questions are not limited to the more readily identifiable forms of bordering religion such as fundamentalism, even believers with a more open and liberal attitude towards other believers do not often raise these questions. The potential conflict that may follow from religious exclusivity appears not to be enough to put the issue on the agenda. Only when religious differences lead to violence, is some attention given to the consequences of diversity. And once the violence is ended, these questions cease to be topical.

What are the implications of the playful approach for this aspect of the bordering position? The framework developed so far suggests that differences between religions are implicit within the huge meaning-making capacity of the human animal. Concrete religions are part of the effort to curtail this wild reflection. Self-reflection and the ability to stand back contribute to the diversity of views. The double experience of belonging and yet standing apart is both the problem and the solution, since by standing back the human animal can consider her (or his) loneliness and think of ways to overcome it, establishing a relationship with the puzzling and challenging wholes that surround her. As was argued, even religion itself will become a whole that confers opportunities to experience belonging.

The role that power mechanisms play can be added to this picture. Power serves to reduce the number of alternatives, endorsing a particular selection from the immense possibilities. A religion, already as a movement and certainly so later on, when institutionalized, will develop its own identity via beliefs and practices. The accompanying power structure protects this identity, internally disciplining believers, externally warding off alternative worldviews. The degree to which this bordering mechanism may happen will vary, but the principle remains more or less the same. Believers may feel frustrated by the strong borders and resist their influence, possibly after experiencing new visions and vocations. As was described, this may be the start of a new cycle. In terms of the two brain hemispheres, there is a delicate relationship between the creative imagination of the right hemisphere and the organizing control of the left, religions and believers taking positions on a spectrum between these poles. The history of religions shows the dynamics of these positions.

The human cost of religious diversity should not be underestimated. Armed conflicts between religious groups are the most noticeable result, including cases where religious differences serve to include or disguise political and economical interests. Samuel P. Huntington's predictions for the twenty-first century give religions the major role in conflicts.[1] Pluralist societies show the difficulties of avoiding such clashes, especially when there appears to be a ritual calendar for armed confrontation, as is the case of Northern Ireland. Meaning-making in religions can produce a strong sense of exclusivity that may include the theocratic goal to bring the world as a whole under one religious leadership. In addition, in the globalizing world, migration streams have created new situations in which people from different religious backgrounds have to live together in one neighborhood. Religious views may come in handy when social inequality and unrest need legitimately to be expressed, as was the case of the Black Muslims and also occurred during the Arab Spring. On the personal level, inter-religious relationships, such as marriages, can cause great affliction to the people involved.

The play perspective could cause a breakthrough in the stalemate that now prevails, opening an alternative to the positions currently available, and reducing the human cost involved. The condition is awareness

1. Huntington, *Clash of Civilizations*.

of the mechanism behind the bordering process, especially the role of domesticated meaning-making and of religious leadership. This demands a certain amount of rethinking, both personally and collectively. This is not impossible, though it may sound utopian. Especially in situations where the authorities, whether secular or religious, do not succeed in developing convincing policy, there is room for the consideration of alternatives. The playful mode of meaning-making, simply by being playful, can be attractive in itself.

The strongest aspect of the playful perspective, however, is that play is a serious affair, contrary to what people often think. This characteristic makes it able to accept diversity, recognizing the seriousness with which believers defend their views, sticking to their own preferred faith. Though there is an element of relativization in the playful approach, once the game is played, each position can be taken seriously, not only by the believer himself (or herself), but also by all those who take different stances—who in turn can be approached in a respectful way. Nobody is asked to renounce his convictions. The only extra dimension that all participants require, is the understanding, especially when tension mounts and human cost is high, that all who play their own religious game, do so seriously, but nevertheless are playing. Humans cannot avoid making meaning. That is their privilege as well as their curse, and they make it in a selective and therefore diverse way. One single meaning they might consider sharing is respect for each other's games. It is a matter of a decisive change in the repertoires of schemas.

Playful awareness need not remain a permanent part of a believer's repertoire. Even liberal believers show bordering tendencies by ignoring the problem of religious diversity. This is understandable and can be pardoned. However, by making the play perspective explicit as soon as conflicts threaten to come out in the open, there may be the opportunity to challenge religions and their believers, both conservatives and liberals, to do what they are good at: that is, to give an idea a ritual form, symbolizing reconciliation, or designing a new common ritual, based on rituals from both sides. This need not even be a new ritual. In fact, the ambiguity of religious repertoires stands a good chance of providing meanings that match the intentions of the playful perspective. If Christians at Pentecost celebrate the Holy Spirit, its creative aspect may be interpreted as an invitation to take a different look at established views in general and start the playful processing of meanings that were in fact the basis for the foundation of any religion.

The playful turn will not arrive overnight. As any change, it needs time and is conditioned. Here is a lesson from the heart of Africa. When doing the fieldwork for my PhD thesis, on boys' initiation ritual in a small tribe on the river Congo, the Wagenia,[2] I discovered that the change in the boys' life obeyed three conditions. In my view these conditions also apply to the playful change I am suggesting. First of all, the change must be social. Even though the initiative may come from an individual, the change affects the whole group, whether of living room dimensions, or a whole society. In the Wagenia case, the whole clan accompanied the boys' transition. The second condition is that the change must be dramatized using clear metaphors. These could possibly be of a ritual nature, but in modern conditions, marketing techniques could be used as well, creating a recognizable logo, and bringing to light significant events. In the Wagenia case the most dramatic symbols were circumcision and confinement in an initiation camp (examples that need not necessarily be followed!). The third condition is a phasing in time, taking one small step after the other, each phase being expressed ritually. The Wagenia boys' initiation ritual could be subdivided into five stages, each with its own symbolism. In any concrete situation, these three conditions can steer creative efforts to accompany and trigger a change, demanding a careful consideration of the social and symbolic aspects, and of the phasing-in process to be followed. The playful attitude may stimulate creativity.

One strong argument for the need to adopt the playful perspective is to reduce the human cost that bordering brings with it, yet still allowing believers to continue to retain their own preferred set of convictions. Once conscious of the causes of human cost, by understanding the demands of the human meaning-making process and of religious power mechanisms, the conclusion can and should be: "Never again." The insight that the serious nature of play has been grossly exaggerated, justifying violence and even death, may cause believers to develop other ways of inter-religious engagement and communication. If efforts are taken to reduce the number of victims through better road and traffic management, why is this approach not taken in inter-religious traffic? The religious game others play can then be a source of inspiration. Their repertoires may contain alternatives to problematic and contradictory views in one's own religion. Simple

2. Droogers, *Dangerous Journey.*

calculation of cost and benefit may be helpful. In many respects the playful approach comes at a small price. It may help prevent Huntington's predictions from coming to fruition.

From the playful point of view, bordering believers need not feel threatened, since they can continue to believe that their worldview is the best. The only change in the bordering schema repertoire is the recognition that their game is one among many, and that it needs a wink from time to time. That gesture alone can reduce the human cost of the bordering phenomenon.

The God Debate

When God is the concept in dispute, the real issue is religion. Atheists ask how people can continue to deceive themselves, maintaining irrational ideas. They wonder how it is possible to believe in entities and beings whose existence cannot be proven scientifically. Religious diversity is interpreted as proof of the absence of absolute truth, since so many absolute truths couldn't exist simultaneously. Besides, do all religions speak of the same sacred beings? Religious persistence is explained by pointing to its many functions, making religion at best a useful illusion. Staunch atheists view believers as being stuck at puberty, refusing to become adults, remaining pre-modern, unaware of the blessings of the Enlightenment and modernization.

As we saw, bordering religions and believers tend to ignore the critique expressed in the God Debate, even when it is part of a public debate that one can't miss. There can be inertia in cultural changes. As long as science was not proclaimed as the most prestigious type of knowledge, the right of religion to exist was not contested. Bordering religions continue and maintain this pre-modern view. In reaction, atheist spokespersons voice their views in a loud and clear manner. To turn a deaf ear to the atheist discourse may be a bordering believer's self-defense, preventing disturbing questions from being asked, but it is also a sign of conviction and self-evidence. Border control will become more vigilant under the impact of these attacks.

Applying the playful perspective, the stalemate between atheists and believers may undergo a breakthrough, changing the frames that both sides use. This perspective suggests that, instead of only looking for differences, one might start looking for common ways of thinking. Those involved on both sides can be shown how they play with meanings. Whether staunch atheist or bordering theist, both suffer from an unbalanced use of the abilities that the divided brain put at the disposition of the human animal, privileging the left hemisphere. Both build systems, in left-oriented style, reducing religious words to their literary meaning, having no right-oriented sense for the fathomless ambiguity of symbols. Both serve power more than play. Atheists tend to lament their minority position and campaign for more power in the public arena, just as fundamentalists do. Bordering, defined in the Introduction in terms of exclusivity and self-sufficiency, is no theist monopoly.

Consequently the current debate is about distorted versions of both atheism and theism, or *mutatis mutandis* of science and religion. Both look at each other from a perverted framework. Both are deluded by exclusive claims that are the consequence of taking versions too seriously. Both claim ultimate answers. On both sides power mechanisms are put to work that reinforce the contrast.

The recovery of the original intention of both is therefore needed. They share the ability to be playful and yet use play without knowing it. In their meaning-making, both create and evoke reality and explore its possibilities, whether they call it God or the Higgs boson, incidentally also called the God particle. As we saw, it is part of the human outfit to be able to develop names and select symbols to make sense of the reality that surrounds the human animal, but we also saw that this selection process can end in a one-sided version.

Obviously there are differences in the way religion and science construct knowledge, science ideally being more self-conscious about the conditions under which sound knowledge emerges. In the God Debate, the difference is made a good deal of, and rightly so. Yet science is not just rational, as if the left hemisphere could suffice. Science can also be portrayed as an intuitive play with possibilities. The results of this game may be reified to final knowledge, as happens when a scientific paradigm is built on the insights of an academic virtuoso, developing an intuition into an institution. As we now know, thanks to Thomas S. Kuhn,[3] paradigm shifts occur, as now seems the case with regard to the Higgs particle. Not all that we now consider certain is made for eternity. This is a consequence of the fact that new scientific ideas are often founded on unproven presuppositions. For innovation, intuition is an important ability. The role of paradigms in scientific practice shows that power is a factor in science as well. Speaking

3. Kuhn, *Structure of Scientific Revolutions.*

in concrete terms, paradigms come with exclusive practices that involve schools, scarce resources, journals, conferences, and public attention. Instead of stimulating innovation, a successful paradigm will tend to impose a model, excluding everything that would falsify it.[4] Some authors who see their articles refused for publication know this. The science game is then played in an over-serious way.

Atheist worldviews lean on an ideal, positivist, and very rational image of science, ignoring the less objective aspects just mentioned, as well as the emergence of other models of science, critical of positivism.[5] Bordering is certainly not exclusive to religion. Secular ideologies moreover have their own presuppositions. One is the belief (!) that society and human beings are manageable, as if there is not a margin of failures. Progress is accordingly accepted as natural and evident. Another presupposition is the belief in the moral goodness of human beings, despite all the atrocities that humans are capable of. Finally the strict rationality of the secular worldview is confessed, despite the role played by the above-mentioned presuppositions.

In their views on religion, atheist critics begin from a particular image of religion that is rather selective. Using theories that explain religion from its functions, they ignore the shortcomings of the functionalist view that were discussed in the previous chapter. They ignore the question of why so many people remain religious, despite what they see as the convincing clarity of the atheist position, just as they do not ask why religions are so diverse and have much more symbolism than would strictly be needed to exercise the functions that atheists and scholars attribute to religion. They also avoid the question of whether these functions have played a role from

4. Here is an example from the cognitive study of religion:

> [T]here has emerged a relatively tightly-knit group of scholars engaged in what has become known as the "cognitive science of religion." This group of scholars enjoys an unusual measure of agreement on shared presuppositions, methods, and problems. Over the last twenty years or so they have succeeded in establishing not only a paradigm for their research, but also several institutional centres around the world, a journal and book series, and a substantial literature based on new empirical research that has given rise to a series of new research problems. Yet despite this institutional success, and their shared sense of conceptual and empirical *progress* in the problems they have set themselves, some social and cultural anthropologists have remained actively resistant to the implications of cognitive research. (Whitehouse and Laidlaw, *Religion, Anthropology, and Cognitive Science*, 13, italics in original.)

5. Guba, *Paradigm Dialog*.

the start, or only in the course of the history of a religion. Moreover, their critique is selective since it targets the gross aberrations that are the consequence of the role of power, especially of the self-serving type, in religion. As I made clear in chapter four, this assessment is correct in itself, but still selective, particularly ignoring the original playful side of religion.

Interestingly, when operating outside the God Debate, staunch opponents may behave in ways that resemble those of believers. They may accept the possibility of psychosomatic causes of afflictions, admitting the prevalence of mind over matter. In choosing their partners they will create an image of the other that may need amending in the course of a person's life history, possibly having serious consequences for the relationship. If they are lovers of art, they would without a qualm accept that artists in their paintings and statues evoke a reality that is as illusory as religious reality. Interestingly, illusory has the same root as the word "ludens" in Homo Ludens, suggesting a link with play. Also in reading novels, critics of religion find it perfectly normal that the author constructs a reality that, as the cover makes clear, is fiction. Yet they may find it "gripping," as if the artificial reality is a reality indeed. They may sacrifice their night rest to continue reading, or on the contrary dare not read on for fear of being faced with a compelling reality they do not desire to know about. Going to the movies, especially to see thriller and horror genre films, but also others, the same posture is accepted as normal. They may go to the opera or a musical and accept that people do not just say what they mean, but, lo and behold, sing it, contrary to ordinary life, and they are full of admiration for what they saw. Enjoying the arts, they will ignore that power is an important aspect of what is presented to the general public, art having its popes and marketing gurus, often causing much ado about nothing. And yet, when it is religion that creates a new reality, this meets with dismay, just as the power mechanisms in religions are the first to be criticized, both the almighty God and his bordering earthly representatives. The usual suspension of disbelief does not function in the case of religion.

Does my appraisal of the atheist position result in religious apologetics? No, the playful approach is a third way, beyond the common opposition. I suggest we leave the trenches behind. In the preceding chapters, I have given my perspective on current religions, most of them deviating from their playful origins, being disciplined by the inevitable machinations of power, just as much located in the left brain hemisphere as atheism is, odd bedfellows finding themselves in similar conditions. Although the modernization process, with its emphasis on the applications of science and technology in society, has set the tone of a contrast between science and religion, one should go beyond that opposition. Atheists and theists could have a dialogue in which they might recognize how both have been deluded by unilateral emphases. The transcendental aspects, always first recognized in religions, are present both in atheist and scientific views of the world, just as they are in art. Since both believer and atheist belong to the species of the human animal, they necessarily depend on ways to control the abundance of meaning-making. The two parties employ different strategies to do so, one using bordering religion as a form of taming the wild reflection, the other trusting in science to do the job. Behind this difference, similarity hides. Coming to a different perception is a matter of selecting other meanings from the plethora available. In both cases, strongly held conviction is rather unfortunate.

Believers, when ready to explore similarity, may discover the rational in their worldviews. Atheists in turn may be surprised by the rationality behind religious system building and the irrationality in their own axioms. Jointly they may become aware that paradigm shifts also occur in religions. In both science and religion, models are built that serve to interpret and understand reality. Atheists and believers use the same brain capabilities, including the risky ambiguity of the brain hemispheres. In their dialogue they may come to understand that both were over-enamored of the possibilities of the left hemisphere, with its utility, clarity, and seductive power-serving bias. They may even come to the conclusion that religion and science have both failed to make the world sufficiently inhabitable. The need for subservient power may be discovered, to reduce the negative impact and human cost of self-serving power.

To summarize, they may take advantage of the following check-list of the new universal ten commandments (with apologies to those bordering believers who may wish to claim the copyright of this format):

1. Discover that all play is a game.

2. Decide that each person should have the liberty to play.

3. Recognize common characteristics.

4. Scrutinize the role of power in each context, especially power of the self-serving type.

5. Encourage forms of subservient power.

6. Explore ways to control the left hemisphere.

7. Rehabilitate the abilities of the right hemisphere.

8. Accept the similarity of basic questions.

9. Explore the role of wholes.

10. Seek to reduce the human cost, learning from previous (mis)rule and (mis)communication.

That seems enough work for the twenty-first century.

Does God Exist?

What does the third way, the playful approach, mean for the concept of God, taken as the central issue in the God Debate? It seems to me that the question of whether God exists has been imposed by the modernization process, that is, by the application of science and technology in society. That process determines our present cultural context. It puts science, and thereby the left brain, in a privileged position, with calamitous consequences, as McGilchrist argues. The modernist view is too optimistic about the production of knowledge. It takes science as the new criterion, nominating it as the judge who will become the uncontested despotic master of his own courthouse. If that judge disagrees with religious affirmations, he is both a party in a conflict and the presiding judge who will decide in his own favor. That position is as biased as that of Christian believers who think that an appeal to the creation story in Genesis is sufficient to condemn Darwin and evolutionism. Some critical perception of one's own images of the other is necessary, as is going beyond stereotypes. It is important to realize that the brain hemispheres make many types of knowledge possible, just as there are many languages and vocabularies, including academic ones. Both hemispheres should be used, in a balanced way. The right hemisphere should keep its leading role.

How to get from under the imposed framework? The liberating message is that play takes the sting out of the discussion, and yet allows both atheists and theists to stick to their convictions and their type of knowledge. Meaning-making is not only a way of rendering reality but also of making it, just as schemas are not only reflections of reality but also contribute to making reality. This is a general human characteristic, shared by believers and atheists alike. Both the abilities and shortcomings of the meaning-making human animal should be acknowledged, in science as well as religion. This makes it henceforth impossible to write truth with a capital T.

Scientists are—ideally—aware of the provisional nature of their find-ings and of the constant need for innovation, though they could be more sensitive to the role of power and paradigm as bordering symptoms in the academic trade. The history of any discipline contains examples of pivotal moments when insights changed radically. After all, "all *knowledge*, partic-ularly scientific knowledge, is no more than an acting 'as if' certain models were, for the time being, true. It is only the left hemisphere that thinks there is certainty to be found anywhere."[6] Large parts of university libraries are therefore outdated, interesting only to the historians of a particular disci-pline, or to the dedicated adherents of the previous paradigm.

Bordering believers, on the other hand, could become more conscious of the tentative nature of religious views, once stripped of the far-reaching influence of especially self-serving power on religious organization and symbolism. To give an example: if the Christian God were called not only Father, but also Mother, as in feminist versions, designed in reaction against male power and symbolism, with all its powerful connotations, does this mean that a totally new God is experienced and proposed? Or is this change proof of the continued effort to express what transcends human comprehension and yet is the raw material of the continued effort to put it in words and metaphors? It is even thinkable that Homo Ludens in the process conceives the idea of a Deus Ludens.[7]

True is what the play with meanings makes plausible and thereby real, as long as the game is played. This is not a form of philosophical idealism. The seriousness of each game protects the authenticity of each worldview. This includes the concept of God, just as it includes its denial. Both believ-ers and unbelievers resemble the character in a Molière play who, to his great amazement, discovers that he has been speaking prose all his life.

McGilchrist has this to say on the term "believe" and the question of God's existence:

> Some people choose to believe in materialism: they act "as if" such
> a philosophy were true. An answer to the question whether God
> exists could only come from my acting "as if" God is, and in this
> way being true to God, and experiencing God (or not, as the case
> might be) as true to me. . . . This acting "as if" is not a sort of

---

6. McGilchrist, *The Master and His Emissary*, 171. Vaihinger, *Philosophy of "As If."*

7. E.g., Michelson, "Deus Ludens." Deus Ludens is also present on Facebook.

cop-out, an admission that "really" one does not believe what one
pretends to believe.[8]

As we saw, Victor W. Turner takes the "as if" as a fundamental characteristic of play.

Both believers and unbelievers should recognize that the origin of
their beliefs is an experimental, tentative quest, testing answers to the basic
existential questions. Incidentally, poetry may be of more use than prose, as
it seems to tell more, despite being less precise, leaving much room for the
reader's meaning-making.[9] The belief in God can be taken as an idea with
which the dimensions can be explored, just as the denial of God's existence
can be an idea to experiment with, both being part of the quest for a meaningful worldview. The serious nature of play serves both.

Should a person conclude that for him (or her) God is a meaningful
reality, then he should have the right to live life accordingly, without people
looking askance at him, just as somebody who comes to the opposite conclusion should have that liberty, without being discriminated against. The
contrast is false, because it denies the central role of wild and subsequently
controlled meaning-making, not yet able to free itself from power mechanisms and discipline. We have far too long been taken hostage by a one-
sided schema, which in its form of meaning-making creates the reality of
a contrast that, when looked at from the play perspective, simply does not
exist. Bordering, sealing "us" off from "them," as it was characterized in the
Introduction, is not just a religious kind of behavior.

If we take the sting out of the God Debate, does all discussion end?
Is there nothing left to disagree about? If each is playful in their own way,
do they leave each other alone? To the contrary, they don't. In view of the
world's problems the dialogue only starts here. Much time will be needed
to clean up all the misunderstandings. The cultural change that is needed
will, as we saw already, take time, demand a social effort, and need a creative dramatic expression. That sets the agenda for the twenty-first century.
One way of organizing this much needed dialogue could be to engage in
role play (!) in which each side takes the point of view of the other, trying to explain that view as clearly as possible. Besides a good laugh, this
will result in a constructive exchange, almost a conversion, changing each
other's convictions. Moreover it is a way, following the Wagenia example,

8. McGilchrist, *The Master and His Emissary*, 170–71.

9. Another reason why I added poems to the chapters.

of dramatizing the change that is supposed to take place, possibly via symbolic means and in a social and phasing-in manner.

Besides showing the relativity of the arguments that are vehemently exchanged in the trench war of the God Debate, the playful approach also puts the discussion about secularization in a different light. The presupposition is the contrast between believing and not-believing. Grace Davie's idea of "believing without belonging"[10] adds another contrast, between belonging and not-belonging, not coinciding with the first contrast. This shows already how ambiguous the concept of secularization is. Secularization is a catchall term. It is used to predict the utter disappearance of religion (in the substantial sense that views religion as focused on the sacred), for the exile of religion to a secluded sector of society or to private life, for the end of religion as a factor in organizing society, and to point to the trend towards people leaving the church or attending irregularly (de-churching). All these meanings of the term come under scrutiny when the playful approach is applied to them. The contrast that is suggested by the presuppositions of the concept, between believing and unbelieving, belonging and not-belonging, loses much of its significance when it becomes evident that whatever the type of meaning-making, religious or not, there is much more similarity than difference. Just as the God Debate was a spin-off of modernization, the secularization thesis was another, marked by a limited schema.

Power

Much has been said already about the role of power processes. Knowing the way things went wrong is a starting-point for improvement. Yet, because of the persistence of power patterns, it is not easy to change established power relations. Those in power are in the best position to maintain their power, self-serving power being the most straightforward substantiation. To show the counterpoint, we will have to make an inventory of actors and factors that are able to change the impasse.

First of all, we need an awareness of how power works. The distinction between self-serving and subservient power can come in handy. The analysis of how the brain hemispheres work has shown how power tends to reduce the view of reality to the perspective from the left hemisphere. Utility being a leading principle, a clear view of cause and effect, in a serial way, shows the way to effective policies, which is typically the leaders' interest.

10. Davie, *Religion in Britain since 1945.*

Bureaucracy has its own rationality. Since power is indispensable, it will always exist. However, precisely for this reason it needs to be controlled. Unregulated, power will fuel itself and make everything else sustain it. The goals at stake must be clearly defined, forcing power back into a facilitating role. Obviously power needs minimal conditions to function, but those in power will always be seduced to use their position to expand their jurisdiction in order to guarantee their continued exercise of power. When this happens, subservient power is transformed into self-serving power. Bordering becomes the rule, usually disguised by reason, law, and tradition.

In the second place, the role of power in religion must be kept in check. We have seen how in the first stage of a religious movement both the scarce nature of the religious experience as well as the difficulty of transmitting its essence to others create opportunities for power to broaden its role. Making this process transparent helps to check for deviation from the subservient ideal. Besides, two criteria for subservient power can be applied. The first is the guarantee that the quality of human life is a core value, never to be given up in the interest of religious power. Killing adversaries is out of the question, as is the use of violence. The second is that power should never put limits on meaning-making. Incidentally, in Romanticism, when the right hemisphere was rehabilitated, it was accepted "that a thing and its opposite may be true."[11] The either/or schema was not popular.[12] Even though power has an indispensable role in making wild meaning-making manageable and practicable, pruning it back to flourish in the future, it should always protect what happens in its margins, instead of eradicating it like weeds, as is the virtually automatic tendency of leadership. If power is of the subservient type, the leadership will have no problems with this criterion. Only self-serving power will be tempted to curb creative meaning-making because it feels threatened by innovative thinking.

Religious power has a special responsibility with regard to secular power. It will tend to seek alliances. However, it may be lured into practices that do not obey the two criteria just formulated. The opposite trend would be a critical attitude towards secular power, as soon as it violates the same two criteria. Religion can serve as the conscience of secular power.

That the vicissitudes of religions show a cyclical pattern may be an aspect that facilitates awareness of the role of bordering and power, including the inevitability of the institutionalization of a successful movement,

11. McGilchrist, *The Master and His Emissary*, 353.

12. Ibid., 363.

engendering self-serving power strategies. The qualities located in the left emissary hemisphere need to remain at the service of the right master hemisphere, especially imagination and cognizance of wholes. A religious virtuoso, taking the initiative for a reform movement, typically uses the right brain hemisphere. In the long run, the balanced use of the hemispheres is the only way for the human animal to survive and enjoy a sustainable existence. It lessens the human cost. Phases of the cycle can be identified.

If the religious environment is characterized more and more by subservient power, this will gradually put an end to the aberrations in the perspectives on the sacred, divinities, and God that are the consequence of self-serving power. If metaphors for the powerful religion and the powerful God become outdated because both religion and society have changed, other meanings can be selected when the experience with the sacred or the divine must be described. Aspects of subservient power will be selected for metaphorical use, pointing to characteristics that have most probably always been there, latent and perhaps also manifest, but marginalized by self-serving tendencies: solidarity, compassion, weakness, vulnerability, equality, availability, service. Religions can start to write new theology, with new perceptions of the sacred and the divine, but also with another type of ethics.[13] In Christianity the theologies of feminism and of liberation are examples of such new approaches, significantly accompanied by the efforts of religious authorities to neutralize their influence. However, if the mentality that this type of new theology propagates becomes part of believers' discourse and practice, atheists will find much less reason to criticize religion, because much of their current discourse focuses on aberrations that correspond with the abuse of power, either attributed to the divinity or to the clergy. Interestingly, the idea of divine power has been criticized by atheists, because that power was not evident, particularly when injustice or atrocities have occurred. According to this reasoning, the notion of almighty power is presupposed to exist, then doubted in view of the presence of human misery and unanswered prayer, ultimately leading to the denial of the existence of the divine altogether. That is how some believers lost their faith and where atheists find contradiction. The only way to go beyond these insolvable options, is to understand the influence of the type of symbolism that self-serving power generates regarding concepts of God. The playful perspective opens the opportunity for this, showing the condi-

13. See Cox, *Feast of Fools*; Appelros, "Playing and Believing"; Appelros, *God in the Act of Reference*; Miller, *Gods and Games*.

tions under which meaning-making takes place. The map can be drawn of the religious and theological landscape between the poles of self-serving and subservient power.

It would seem that individualization, as a byproduct of modernization, has changed the prevalent power structure. If the individual person becomes the focal point of a culture, those in power positions have to reckon with this. The emphasis on rationality has served to legitimate the person's right to individuality. As far as politics are concerned, democracy has stimulated individual responsibility and has made positions of power less absolute, which makes politicians nervous when election time approaches. Similarly, in the religious field, the Reformation had already rehabilitated the individual believer's experience and his decision to choose the religion of his preference, turning conversion into a decisive moment, also changing views on salvation. New religions such as Pentecostalism,[14] but also the New Age,[15] are strong examples of religions for the rehabilitated individual, combining emotional and rational elements in an interesting way. So modernization could be hailed as the liberator of the individual believer, not just within one religion, but also facilitating her or his exit to other religions and even from religion altogether. It would seem that this has greatly improved the climate for playful religion, with the limitations imposed by power being eroded.

However, McGilchrist[16] makes a relevant observation, tempering possible optimism. Individuality can indeed incite a search for the original, deviating from the conventional. Yet, in his view, much depends on the way individuality is interpreted by each of the brain hemispheres. As we saw already "the right hemisphere's orientation is towards experience of the Other, whatever it is, the world in as much as it exists apart from the mind." The left hemisphere, on the contrary, has "its own coherent system derived from what the right hemisphere makes available to it, but which is essentially closed." Consequently "[w]e see ourselves as separate: in the right-hemisphere case, still in vital connection with the world around us; in the left-hemisphere case . . . isolated, atomistic, powerful, competitive." These affirmations also apply to individuality in religious matters. They show that individualization must not be understood as the opposite of the

14. Anderson, *Studying Global Pentecostalism*.

15. Kemp and Lewis, *Handbook of New Age*.

16. All quotes in this paragraph are from McGilchrist, *The Master and His Emissary*, 309.

social. In processes of modern individualization, social elements remain active in a variety of ways. Consequently, as McGilchrist suggests, there are options with regard to the individual's position. Individualization is not by definition the rescue of the playful believer from the jaws of bordering self-serving power. The characteristics that McGilchrist attributes to the left-hemisphere can in fact be recognized in self-serving religious power. It is just a matter of which version of individualization is selected. In instances where individualization is not just a matter of the emissary left hemisphere and the qualities associated with it in the right master mind prevailing, believers of old and new religions may use their individuality to be "in vital connection with the world" and oriented "towards experience of the Other."

The practice of the individualist new religions just mentioned, Pentecostalism and New Age, may serve as an illustration of the options, allowing for both the master's and the emissary's emphases, open or closed to the world, connected or isolated, compassionate or ego-centered, lived experience or standardized routine, deep understanding or strict doctrine, question or answer, subservient or self-serving. This will become visible in the concrete form that adherents of a new religion give to their conviction. Interestingly, these new religions open room for emotional behavior and extra-sensorial experiences and moreover cater to individual needs. Their adherents thus are in a position to rediscover the sources of religion, re-constructing the situation that prevailed before self-serving power imposed itself. They may then even seek the conversion of their religious leaders, instead of leaders seeking to convert new believers.

In any religion, lay believers could demand that the leadership obey the criteria of subservient power that were just summarized. Even when these values do not convince people right away, their low human cost could be a reason for the powerful to change their leadership style. Since any religion disposes of a huge repertoire of meanings, it will not be too difficult to find supporting texts in holy scriptures or articles of faith to justify the playful approach. That may be the start of a different, unfettered religious game.

The Four Global Problems

How can the approach developed in this book be of assistance when seeking to solve the four global problems of *poverty, violence, pollution,* and *conflict*? And what role could religions play in the process? As we saw, the peculiar problem is that religions can be said to contribute to the causes as well as the solutions. The good news is that religions potentially possess all the assets needed to engage in the solution to these problems. The bad news is that the perseverance and tenacity of self-serving power frustrates such efforts. This double and contrary identity is in part the consequence of religions' ambiguity with regard to power. Examples of the effect of subservient and self-serving power can be found in the history of religions as well as in their current attitude. Power positions serve to inspire and maintain worldviews that directly relate to the four problems. Whether attributed to minority groups or central to the majoritarian leadership, the weighty question of the double identity is often repressed. As long as this is the case, atheists are right in criticizing religions. The effect of the bordering process is moreover that religions can permit themselves to be deaf to criticism relating to their negative or passive role. Whereas the urgency of the call for a sustainable earth is now understood by many, religions can hardly be taken to task for their ambiguous stance. The playful approach serves to take a fresh look at this barrier on the way to a sustainable earth.

In thinking about religions' attitude towards the four problems, it is clear that the religions and leaderships differ in relation to the degree to which they cause the four problems to occur or help to solve them. Moreover, each of the four problems has its own conditions and accordingly the role that religions play differs with each problem. Yet the four problem areas are also connected, and this may appear in the religious points of view. If, for example, the polluted earth is not able to sustain its population, poverty will be rampant and violent conflicts over scarce resources will break out. One need not accept Huntington's rather essentialist views on the role of religion in twenty-first-century conflicts to admit that religions are important actors in the current situation.

The map of the ambiguity in religious meaning-making concerning these four problems can be sketched more concretely. Thus one may think of religious ideas that justify *poverty* as a divine punishment, as the consequence of the moral quality of a person in an earlier life, as a test of a person's faith and fidelity, as a moral lesson in modesty, as a welcome renunciation of earthly pleasures, or as an opportunity to control greed. On the other hand, religions also promote values that are meant to diminish poverty, such as giving alms. Wealth may be viewed as a risk instead of as a blessing. Equality before the divine may be translated into horizontal relations between believers.

Violence can both be condemned and encouraged by religious points of view. It is, of course, closely connected to the type of power, the self-serving powers being more ready to justify it when it seems useful in maintaining their position and in realizing their religion's goals and interests. Holy wars and violent crusades have thus been legitimated. At the same time violence can be condemned or at least restricted. Sacrifice can take the form of submission to violence.

Though *pollution* may seem a more secular problem, religious pollution being limited to the supposedly impure status of certain people at certain moments, the basic attitude of a religion can be to consider nature as a divine gift to humans who are allowed to make use of it as they like. This may be expressed in creation myths, especially in certain understandings of human beings as the crown of creation. The counterpoint is the call to act responsibly and show respect. The task to defend life may include other animals, saving them from extinction.

Finally, *conflicts* can draw in two religious parties, but secular interests may be at stake as well, possibly being legitimated in a religious manner. Religious differences can be emphasized to such a degree that conflict is viewed as the only remaining action. Expansion as a core value can also legitimate conflict. This may take theocratic forms, bringing global society under a religion's rule. Such views can be found in Christian and Muslim minority groups, having a blueprint for the new society and its laws. Here as well contrary values can also be promoted, religions demanding that conflicts be avoided, urging believers to act in a peaceful way. All in all, as a consequence of religious ambiguity, the human cost is both increased and reduced. Exclusivity and inclusivity are both represented.

This summary shows that ambiguity may be problematic, but it also contains the components of a different attitude. In some way, all four global problems have a power dimension that may be instrumental in both causing human cost and preventing it, with the self-serving and subservient types of power in their familiar roles. What can the playful approach do to constrain the negative effects and to make believers select the positive meanings from their repertoires? Several of the aspects discussed so far in this chapter may be referred to in this context as well. What was said about religious diversity applies here too, not only with regard to conflicts, but also where the need for religions to join forces is concerned. Although diversity may be thought to prevent inter-religious cooperation, when approached in a playful manner it may stimulate the common quest for solutions, taking the diversity not as a handicap but as an asset. The spectrum of ideas and practices, especially of the positive kind, may inspire believers to learn from each other and to cooperate. The insight that all religions represent games in which believers play with possibilities and answers may bring a decisive change in attitude. The transformation of religious power from self-serving to subservient will contribute to such a change, since much less apology and defense is needed. Even the distinction between believers and atheists may lose its significance when perceived from the playful perspective, making cooperation much easier. The right-hemispheric focus on wholes and imagination may serve as a counterweight against the left-hemispheric focus on utility and power.

It is obvious that religious leaders need to "change their mind" if the selection of positive meanings that inspire the answer to global problems is to contribute in any way. Believers are also important, being able to convince their leaders to take responsibility. If the leadership prefers the subservient type of power, this will not be too difficult, especially if the clerics have themselves already discovered the potential of their religious heritage viewed from the playful perspective. If self-serving tendencies are still active, it will be much more difficult to change the leaders' views, because they cannot be approached easily. Besides, leaders often have to operate as managers, leaving reflection to a special class of experts, such as theologians. If a playful theology is developed, within the concrete setting of a particular religion, the chances to "convert" the leadership will increase. Though a divine mission, conversion can be a devil of a job.

Religious Education the Playful Way

Any religious educator, whether working with children or adults, volunteer or professional, will have sensed already that the playful approach has consequences for her or his line of work. Educational work with children may be expected to come with an advantage, since they are still playful, sometimes more than the teacher or moderator would welcome. To be educated may mean that children learn to control their playfulness, making room for seriousness as a step on the path to adulthood. Gradually the left hemisphere begins to play its role, putting limits on the right hemisphere's experiences. Yet, while still playful, children are able to raise surprisingly good questions and also come up with remarkable answers. Not yet fully conditioned, they are still sufficiently spontaneous to explore possible themes, uncovering new dimensions of meaning-making. Nothing should be labeled a silly question. The fishermen's children in Márquez's story who discovered the drowned man's corpse were still in their explorative phase. Even adolescents, precisely because they are rebellious, may seek to test adult certainties, experimenting with alternatives. Their input into discussions should not be dismissed as immature or heretical. Children are able to do what adults have unlearned. From the playful perspective, roles may be inverted, children becoming their educators' teachers. For adult education this means that de-conditioning is more important than further conditioning in terms of a religion's beliefs and practices. In short, we should aspire to becoming like a child, as one founder of a world religion put it.[17]

Religious education itself may therefore serve as the field where the delicate tension between power and play can be explored. The fact that education is the goal of the contact introduces a vertical element, although this may be given a minimal form, more subservient than self-serving. The educational context is a laboratory for experiments with subservient power. The educational relationship thus already offers an opportunity to experiment with new forms of power in the contact between believers. In addition, the transmission of beliefs and practices of a religion may be used to rethink the established views on religion, power, and play. The playful perspective developed in this book may serve as the framework for such a new approach.

The weighty questions discussed in this chapter, especially when traditionally ignored, can be taken as starting-points, making the abstract model more concrete. Several of these questions may come up, once youngsters or new converts begin discovering what their faith is about. The questions that atheists raise may very well be theirs as well. The playful approach offers the potential to take a fresh look at the standard answers, if there are answers. The two criteria that are meant to prevent power from shifting from subservient to self-serving goals, that is, the quality of human life and the freedom for meaning-making, can be explained, trained, and applied to the concrete context of the religious group.

Then, to discuss the four questions, *religious diversity* can be looked at anew, without bordering tendencies, yet presenting the game played in this religion as a serious possibility. The *God Debate* may be a topic that stimulates new discussions on the prevalent concept of God, showing that the difficulty of defining the divine is at the same time an opportunity

17. Matt 18:3.

141

to find new ways of expressing believers' experience with the sacred and appreciating other religions' efforts in this respect. With regard to *power*, religious education can teach the difference between subservient and self-serving power, most probably selecting insights from the religion's heritage in scriptures and oral traditions. Each of the four *global problems* represents a challenge to the usual positions taken in a religion, every time asking whether religion takes the role of cause or solution. Though poverty, violence, and pollution are important issues, the matter of conflict is highly relevant to religions and could be submitted to a reappraisal from the playful perspective.

Moreover, though not necessarily part of the content for discussion, educators may keep in mind what McGilchrist had to say about the possible lack of balance between the two brain hemispheres. The educational situation offers a good opportunity to stimulate the right hemisphere when the educated are still exploring the possibilities. Though conditioning may be an educator's goal, as we saw, de-conditioning is an important element in the playful approach, and this may mean that the dominant role of the left hemisphere in building a system and imposing it on new believers needs to be criticized. The tendency in education towards serial verbalization and rational argument may also need to be reconsidered.

This approach to religious education may meet with resistance in bordering religions of the conservative and fundamentalist types. The playful approach may not just prove to be a bridge too far, but may simply be unthinkable. When, as we saw, self-serving power prevents discussions on weighty questions, it is very improbable that the posture advocated in this book will take root. The room to play won't exist. Yet, the over-serious urge to reflect on one's own tradition may include the consideration of alternative meanings, if only in order to reject them. The zealous desire to be an exemplary believer may bring a person in contact with critical questions, precisely because of his apologetic and polemical attitude. Although the margins are small, renewal may still be possible. As we saw, current fundamentalism can be interpreted as being stimulated by modernization, and as a reaction to some of its consequences. Similarly, a change in conditions may challenge bordering believers and their leaders to change their repertoires. Here too the slogan is "never say never."

In the most succinct way possible, religious education from the playful perspective can be viewed as a stimulant to the promotion of a playful attitude in future generations. If the established religion is a corrupted form of religion, degenerated by power mechanisms that have even altered the contents and symbolism of the faith, the task of religious educators is immense. In fact, before anyone else, the religious leadership itself should be the target group. Though this boils down to no less than revolution, the careful reappraisal of long-forgotten repressed meanings in a religion's repertoires may serve to convert the leaders. Moreover, the human cost involved in current practices and beliefs can be put forward as an argument to change policies in a radical way. This may be the start of a playful revival or reformation, making a religion ready for the future, and moreover contributing to the solution of global problems. Educators are in a position to take the initiative and to develop methods and programs to reach this result.

The New Study of Religion[18]

The playful approach offers an explanation of religion, and hopefully it will be added to the scholarly repertoire in the study of religion. I might stop here, and the reader who is not involved in the study of religion may indeed feel free to skip this section. Yet, in finishing this chapter there are a number of reasons to consider the implications of the playful approach for the study of religion as a discipline. In view of the human cost, an examination of bordering processes should be an important priority.

Thus, the inclusion of power in the model developed here suggests that students of religion may reconsider their usual position of the objective outsider, watching religious turmoil unfold from a safe distance. The scholar may be said to have power in his (or her) field of study, with which he acts as architect and director, at least of his own version of that field. A scholar is an academic entrepreneur. The results of his research on the role of power in religions may serve as a kind of power in policy-making. He may moreover have experienced that power is part of his academic environment, himself and his interpretation occupying a position in the force field. The playful perspective includes the scholar, with his discipline's special way of making sense of believers' ways of making sense of their lives. His game is a meta-game, playing with believers' games and academic games. Furthermore, power and play may seem neutral phenomena and objective concepts, but together they introduce, as suggested

18. Parts of this section contain insights published before in Droogers, "Towards the Concerned Study of Religion." See also Droogers and Van Harskamp, *Methods for the Study of Religious Change.*

in this book, a tension that mirrors the human animal's fundamental oscillation between wild and domesticated meaning-making. In the case of self-serving power, the tension increases, with strong bordering tendencies resulting from it, threatening both free meaning-making and quality of life. Again, from his own work the scholar may be acquainted with self-serving power that directs his way of meaning-making and reduces the quality of his academic life, for example when nobody wants to publish his brilliant new ideas. Outside the academic arena, the urgency of the four global problems just discussed puts the study of religion in a different context. Adding to this the views that McGilchrist developed regarding the lack of balance between the hemispheres of the brain and the link between the brain, religion, and science, the student of religion may feel intrigued with that aspect of the playful approach as well. In sum, whatever his version of the discipline or his walk of life, the scholar in the field of religion is challenged to make these various concerns explicit and to develop an engaging framework for himself and his work. As shown earlier in this section, this change in attitude will alter his way of doing their job, consequently altering the identity of their discipline, making it much more applied. So this book is not just about believers, it also includes the people who study them. Here is a programmatic profile of the reinvented study of religion, successively presenting *theoretical framework, themes, methodology, and research infrastructure.*

The *theoretical framework* focuses attention on the role of power and play in religion. These concepts are interpreted as part of the human predicament, humans simultaneously searching for meaning in an unlimited way (play) and yet controlling this capacity to make it applicable in social contexts (power). This paradox finds its physical basis in the brain hemispheres. Believers and scholars share this human framework, each submitted to its potential and its limitations, each dealing with power and play, including the disparity—and possible parity—between the two. Power manifests itself on a spectrum between the self-serving and subservient poles. The transition zone between the two types, that is, the area where bordering begins occurring, can be determined by applying the two criteria regarding the quality of human life and free meaning-making. The abilities of the two brain hemispheres correspond to this spectrum.

With regard to the *themes* in the discipline's research agenda, the applicability of knowledge obtained in research is important. Although the power context is not new, nowadays the globalization process gives it an unprecedented dimension. This is visible in the four global problems of poverty, violence, pollution, conflict, which lend urgency and applicability to the theoretical approach and to thematic choices. In choosing concrete themes, priority is therefore given to research on the role of power and play in bordering processes, with special attention given to religions' position where the four problems are concerned. In view of the fact that not only religions, but ideologies and other secular worldviews operate in this arena as well, the themes studied should be expanded to include these positions and their role. Religious studies must therefore be transformed into worldview studies. Research results must not be kept locked within academia, but will, in view of their applied nature, serve to provide crucial input for policy-makers and for inter-religious contacts and dialogue. Although inter-religious encounter is in itself a relevant topic, major attention is to be given to the global problems mentioned, also as a topic for dialogue. Research themes may also be chosen in the light of McGilchrist's thesis about the unbalanced use of the hemispheres of the brain in which the roles of master and emissary tend to be inverted.

With regard to *methodology*, the usual research strategies can continue to be used, yet with adaptations in the function of the applicability of results. The engaged position of the researcher will lead to increased interest in participant observation, and to a less distant and more "subjective" position. Insights into the way power works may imply that the researcher takes sides and puts his abilities at the service of those who suffer under self-serving power and, on the other hand, stimulating efforts to promote subservient power. This may result in forms of so-called "action research" also called "advocacy research."[19] The criticism of the dominance of the left brain may result in methodological choices for methods that rest on the abilities of the right hemisphere. This includes a rehabilitation of qualitative methods, albeit in combination with quantitative methods based on left-hemispheric abilities.

Moreover, an experiment with both transcendentalist and naturalist perspectives, discussed in chapter three, becomes possible. Play inspires a special methodological position, what I call "methodological ludism."[20] This strategy follows from the similarity between believer and researcher, as distinguished from the contrast between religion and science, which has received most attention. To the degree that the supposed scientific posture

19. Huizer and Mannheim, *The Politics of Anthropology*. Trotter and Schensul, "Methods in Applied Anthropology."

20. For further reading see Droogers, "Methodological Ludism," and *Play and Power in Religion*, 311–64. Also, Knibbe and Droogers, "Methodological Ludism."

reduces the researcher's possibility to understand religion from within, there is a need for a bridging method. Methodological ludism refers to the researcher's attitude of a double framework, related to the definition of play as the capacity to deal simultaneously with two ways of classifying reality. This playful attitude applies the double approach to religion, first of all to religion as an object of study, but also to the study of religion, in an effort to combine the scientific and religious perspectives. The researcher looks at religion from within, from the believer's standpoint, if only for ten seconds, but for long enough to understand the religious view. This method is especially recommended to skeptical researchers who consider themselves secularized, yet are fascinated by the persistence of religion. Methodological ludism goes beyond the usually distinguished positions of methodological theism (the sacred reality exists), atheism (that reality does not exist), and agnosticism (there is no certainty as to the existence of sacred reality). It also combines the transcendentalist and naturalist positions. Methodological ludism will help discover the role of play in religion, since a quality of the object of research is used in the method used to study it.

Finally, the new profile has consequences for the *infrastructure* of the field of study. Awareness of the role of power and of the urgency of applied research will in the long run, and hopefully also in the short run, have consequences for the organization of research on religion. Funding policies need to adapt if the analysis developed so far makes sense. The criteria for application will change accordingly. When funds are spent on comprehensive research programs, more than on individual grants, the choice of overarching themes will change accordingly, as in fact is already happening. Funding agencies, applicants, and reviewers will all adapt their conduct. Recent examples of this include the programs of the Dutch Humanities Research Council, with the title "The Future of the Religious Past,"[21] and of NORFACE, a joint venture of European research councils, on the question of the "Re-emergence of Religion as a Social Force in Europe." Politicians may discover the relevance of research on bordering processes and on global problems, and invest money in it. A more applied perspective will also have an impact on the ways in which scholars communicate the results of their research, in journals, conferences, and book series, all often linked to—sometimes powerful—associations or networks of like-minded scholars. This revision of the infrastructure will take time to occur. As any

---

21. The project resulted so far in three edited volumes, in chronological order: Vries, *Religion: Beyond a Concept*; Borg and Henten, *Powers*; and Houtman and Meyer, *Things*.

culture, academic sub-cultures are slow to change, though—as we saw—dramatization, phasing-in, and socializing can speed up the process. The urgency of the problems that the applied study of religion—or better still, of worldviews in general—finds on its agenda may also help to rapidly set a new course.

Conclusion

In this final chapter we could harvest what the playful approach, developed in the preceding chapters, confers with regard to the very concrete weighty questions that bordering religions and believers tend to ignore. Each of the four questions allowed us to show the relevance of the playful perspective for understanding the bordering process. These problems are to a large degree connected with each other, power having a pivotal role, which reinforces their impact. Their wide presence and broad implications make the urgency of the matter palpable. Going beyond mere comprehension, the playful frame of mind therefore incites us to make the research results from the study of religion applicable, thus ultimately reducing the human cost that the bordering phenomenon brings with it. Scientific meaning-making has its limitless tendencies as well, addressing any conceivable topic. Yet, some control may come from the need to offer humanity a sustainable future. Though unable to avoid wishful thinking and utopian optimism, the play model provides us with concrete tools to generate better kinds of management and policy, also relevant to the field of religion and religions. As has happened in the past when cultures and policies changed, the calculation of the human cost involved can be the catalyst for significant change. This provides a stronger argument than everything else put forward in this book.

The Divine Image — A Song of Innocence

To Mercy Pity Peace, and Love,
All pray in their distress,
And to these virtues of delight
Return their thankfulness.

For Mercy Pity Peace and Love,
Is God our father dear,
And Mercy Pity Peace and Love,
Is Man his child and care.

For Mercy has a human heart,
Pity, a human face,
And Love, the human form divine,
And Peace, the human dress.

Then every man of every clime,
That prays in his distress,
Prays to the human form divine,
Love Mercy Pity Peace.

And all must love the human form,
In heathen, turk or jew;
Where Mercy Love & Pity dwell
There God is dwelling too.

—*William Blake*

Conclusion

DE-BORDERING

Looking back

WHAT HAS THIS LONG exercise brought us? What did we learn about bordering religions? From where does the tendency come to treat the results of a group's meaning-making activities as exclusive and self-evident? And how can playful religion become an alternative to this tendency? To answer these questions, a rather complex picture has been drawn in this book, combining a variety of elements and insights. Though strictly speaking going beyond the theme of bordering religions, the discussion needed to be broadened to locate bordering religions within a wider framework.

The human animal is the tragic main character in the picture that was painted here. Her (or his) huge brain power is not just a blessing, but also a curse. Her efforts at reflection are supposed to discover the sense in reality, but even with a wealth of possibilities, reality escapes her understanding. A set of wholes remains beyond her control. Religion was presented as one of the ways to compensate for her failure to manage these wholes, and moreover to tame the human animal's endless and restless desire for reflection. A religion's answers to the five basic questions that any worldview seeks to answer, pertaining to death, morals, truth, beauty, and identity, suggest the existence of a regained order, putting an end to upsurges of the inchoate.

The modernization process, which for two centuries has brought drastic changes to world society, applying the results of science and technology, radically transforming human life in all its aspects, is the landscape in which I picture the modern human animal. Under modernization the already abundant human capacity for reflection expanded in a way never shown before, in science and technology, but as a consequence also in many other sectors of human life. This made the human animal even more tragic, since she or he has difficulty in managing this huge change in scale and complexity. Global society is accordingly faced with a number of problems: poverty, violence, pollution, and conflict.

The transformed environment altered religions' roles. Religious knowledge now had to compete with scientific knowledge. Atheism entered the public domain. With regard to the global problems, many religions proved to act ambiguously, both causing and solving these problems.

A special feature of the picture of the human animal stems from the notions of power and play, which lend a twisted effect. Power serves the taming of the human animal's wild meaning-making since it radically reduces the number of behavioral alternatives. Play works in precisely the opposite direction, allowing for more ways of classifying reality. Play and power are therefore at loggerheads with each other, two souls at war within the human breast. This battlefield between the two extremes knows a variety of positions. Cultures, societies, religions, and eras differ in this respect. In order to understand concrete situations, I introduced the distinction between subservient and self-serving power. Two criteria help to determine which type prevails: the quality of life and the freedom of meaning-making. It is also important to see that play demands a serious attitude and that this characteristic allows for the entry of power into play territory, seriousness—without play—often being the survivor. However, it is the margin, far from the power center, that was shown to be the preferred play center.

The picture of the human animal was given a special color by applying insights from some sectors of cognitive studies. Her (or his) tragic fate of being a wild meaning-maker, who fails in her job and whose playfulness is domesticated by power mechanisms, proved to be afflicted by tense relations between the hemispheres of the brain. The respective qualities of the right and left sides correspond roughly with the playful and the powerful, the seekers and the established, the wanderer and the *arrivé*. The ludic is making the human animal either lucid (the right perspective) or ludicrous (the left view). Though the right hemisphere is supposed to be the master and the left the emissary, the latter exploits, as a real sorcerer's apprentice, any opportunity to behave as the master. Whereas the Enlightenment has created such an opportunity through the modernization process, in religions the dominance of the left hemisphere can be shown to have existed as long as institutionalization has taken place, especially when leading to the self-serving type of the exercise of power, including the exclusivity and insularity that typify bordering processes. Religious playfulness has thus long been sacrificed on power's altar. Another cognitive addition was the concept of schema repertoire, illuminating the dynamics of meaning-making.

Seemingly, modernization brought the individual's freedom, restricting power's action-radius. This would create chances for playful meaning-making, but there are counter forces at work too. Power and the left hemisphere of the brain have their own versions of the free individual. Moreover, modernization and globalization produce a complex mix of free and yet constrained choice.

Where do bordering processes appear in the portrait of the human animal? What does he (or she) look like if he is an adherent of a bordering religion? Especially when they display symptoms of the self-serving type of power, bordering religions help tame the wild and playful meaning-maker. They offer their believer a clear and limited interpretation of human reality that eliminates the threat of uncontrolled wholes. He receives plausible and exclusive answers to the five basic worldview questions, the doctrinal and social structures reinforcing each other. He does not have access to alternatives. Border control is combined with strong institutionalization, hierarchy, and inner discipline. On the spectrum between power and play the average bordering believer finds himself much closer to the power pole than to that of play. His leaders pay lip service to the criteria that guarantee quality of life and freedom of meaning-making, reformulate them to match the prevailing system, or ignore them. The margins for change are narrow or non-existent. In cognitive terms, bordering religions use rather closed schema repertoires that reflect the role of the left brain hemisphere in system building and that show neglect of the right half. Bordering religions react to modernization by strengthening their position. The believer is protected against inconvenient new questions, even when they seem weighty, such as those relating to the existence of other religions, atheistic questions, the role of power in the institution, and religion's role in the above-mentioned global problems. The effect is that human cost is relatively high, especially when the bordering religion is also a power in society. For his sense of security the believer pays high port charges for moorings in a safe harbor, to be used during stormy periods.

In terms of our definition provided in the Introduction, bordering is not an exclusively religious characteristic. The tendency to treat the results of a group's or a category's meaning-making activities as exclusive and self-evident can be found outside religion as well. Virtually all traits in the bordering believer's portrait may appear in the picture of somebody with a secular worldview. Though not necessarily organized within a group, occupying a less powerful position in society, she (or he) may be as exclusive and self-sufficient as a believer in a bordering religion. Her views on power are determined by her exclusive minority position. Instead of religion, science serves to tame wild and playful meaning-making. Modernization is the secular person's ally, not her enemy, as is the case of the strict bordering believer. The secularization thesis, predicting religion's defeat, nourished her hopes for the future. The answers to the five basic questions reflect her strong convictions. Her systematic worldview is primarily a left-hemisphere product. Belonging to a minority, she dreams of becoming part of a majority and a force in public life.

Is there a way to convert the bordering adherent, whether of a religious or a secular worldview? Would it be possible to paint the portrait of this convert and recommend playful behavior? Before addressing the convert in a letter, we must take a look at the role of the *u-ass*, short for *unproven assumption*, since this may be the catalyst of the bordering adherent's conversion process. It is also another brushstroke on the bordering human animal's picture.

The U-ass

As we saw, the enormous ability for meaning-making has unwieldy aspects. Too much is thinkable and nevertheless full control of reality and its opacity has proven to be impossible. An important instrument is the u-ass. The u-ass is unproven, but treated as real and true, thereby creating the illusion of control. It serves as the safety valve, diminishing the pressure on the human animal. The human animal, being a product of devolution, having fallen upwards, is an illusion-consuming animal who for her (or his) survival feeds on u-asses. Her mode of survival is to deceive herself. Using u-asses as default assumptions, her handicap has been transformed into a challenge. She was seeing herself "through a glass, darkly," "a poor reflection as in a mirror,"[1] but most happily in the end she observes herself face to face. "Mirror, mirror on the wall, despite everything, I am the most beautiful of them all." A hunch is always better than ignorance, conjecture

---

1. 1 Cor 13:12.

better than empty hands. If not everything can be proven, u-asses become perfectly acceptable.

The person's or culture's set of u-asses serves to keep a sense of failure away. If we no longer accept our u-asses, we need psychiatric care. If the human animal is strong on meaning-making, yet discovering the inbuilt limitations, his or her playful energy is best invested in u-asses. The only condition is to forget that it is unproven. It should not be criticized. The u-ass is the compromise between the brain hemispheres, being the product of the exploring right hemisphere, subsequently accepted by the left hemisphere that looks the other way. In its hunger for clarity, utility and impact, the left half treats the u-ass as a p-ass, a proven assumption, passed into the system that it builds. Though his oversized brain is his handicap, the human animal succeeds in living with it, simply by using it to develop u-asses. For being effective, u-asses are taken seriously, despite their playful origins—which are consequently forgotten since they remind one of the unproven nature of u-asses. The biggest u-ass of all is that our behavior is rational and consistent, and that u-asses are for the dumb only.

This rather abstract and general formulation can be complemented with a series of examples, first profane, then religious. In the secular sphere, presuppositions steer our social relations. Society is a big u-ass game, each society with its own repertoire of u-asses. Those in power control and maintain that repertoire. When moving to another state or country, we have to discover the local u-asses. If two people in conversation use the same word, the u-ass is that they understand that term in the same way. Belief in the goodness of humans is a widespread u-ass, as is the possibility of moral purity. We assume that there is good will in the people we meet, although we also sometimes are on our guard with particular categories of other people, even without class or ethnic prejudice. Some people are reticent towards uniformed policemen, others with gentlemen in Italian suits who wear dark glasses. Democracy has its u-asses as well, such as the idea that all voters have sufficient knowledge of the candidates and their programs to be able to vote in a responsible way, or that the winner is the best candidate. Authorities may enjoy the support of u-asses, such as when people automatically trust those they elected to an office, perhaps until proof of that person's ineptitude comes to light. Loneliness can be overcome by the u-ass of belonging as the rule. Despite statistical evidence that we may choose our partner from among millions of people, we apply the u-asses of being in love and of eternal fidelity in our relationship with that one person.

Gender relations are marked by u-asses. We also tend to believe that deep down we remain the same self all our life, despite the constant changes in our identity, almost by the hour. A complementary u-ass is the autonomy of the self. Modernization has put the individual self in the center, supposing that the self has all the qualities needed to fulfill its role—another u-ass. Free will is another example, as is continuous progress. Before the crisis a widely held u-ass was that economists and bankers were in control of the economy and that the market regulates itself. Science is not without u-asses, which serve as axioms. Paradigms are based on u-asses, often ignored, until contested. A popular u-ass in scholarly debate is that arguments convince. Among atheists a popular u-ass is that only religious people have u-asses.

Religion indeed has its u-asses, but it does not hold the monopoly. Yet they are abundantly present here as well. Thus the women of the fishermen's village in Márquez's story reconstructed Esteban's life during their vigil, in spite of the lack of any evidence, but to them it seemed sufficiently convincing. My own experience, after grandson Sam's stillbirth, with the butterfly in our garden, brought consolation, but again this amounts to consolation without proof. An important u-ass in religion is that what can be imagined also can be real, even when not endorsed by empirical reality. Accordingly, the main u-ass is the existence of the sacred or the divine, including its availability for communication and mystical contact. The experience of uncontrollable wholes inspires the concept of a sacred, or divine Other. The imagination reifies it into reality. Dreams and visions nourish u-asses. Then a world created from an egg, or a goddess with many arms becomes possible and real. Metaphors suggest links between domains that are normally not connected. The same ability to make the symbols that sets the human animal apart, at a distance from reality, serves to design a world of which she or he can feel part. A feeling of belonging and togetherness, of being part of a larger whole, becomes a central religious u-ass. A complementary u-ass is the control that the believers regain over the sacred or divine. The sacred's manifestation is experienced, or has become part of tradition, transmitted from one generation to the next. Religious leadership protects and promotes its preferred repertoire of u-asses. An important u-ass is that there is only one truth, to be found in one religion. Socialization makes the u-asses acceptable. Once the game is played in a serious manner, playfulness does not worry about proof. Most believers accept this presupposition, although they may have doubts as well. The u-asses are legitimated by sacred or divine confirmation. Religions teach us how to whistle against fierce gusts of wind.

A classic anthropological example of the role of u-asses is that of Quesalid, a critical Kwakiutl (West-Canada) described by Franz Boas, whose case was analyzed by Claude Lévi-Strauss.[2] Not believing in the sorcerers' capacities and out of sheer curiosity, Quesalid became a pupil of one of them. His worst suspicions were confirmed. Yet, when a sick person, who had dreamed that Quesalid was to help him, called upon him, the treatment he gave was successful. That was the start of his triumphant career as a sorcerer. The fact that the u-ass worked, although unproven, convinced him. Though critical of others, he from then on defended his own methods, feeling validated by his successes.

U-asses are indispensable in the life of the human animal, whether religious or atheist. They appear in many sectors without being noticed, which is all the better for their functioning. They should go unobserved. The consequence is that we remain unaware of the role of play in our way of life. And in fact, since play must be done in a serious manner, we should engage in the game, without always being conscious that we are playing. Reflection about the origin and the role of u-asses is lethal.

So my advice to the reader is: you were so kind as to bear with me till this page, learning about the role of play, but please forget what you picked up here, just play the game, and do it in a serious manner! Yet, before I finish and shut up about play, I would like to address the converted de-bordered player, by writing him (or her) a letter, to present along with his portrait as I would paint it. This is my way of translating a general and rather abstract argument onto the concrete universe of one person. It also shows how the playful approach can be applied. It is my short guide for the road, from the powerful to the playful religion.

Dear De-bordered Player, Dear Illusion Animal,

At the beginning of this century, HBO produced two seasons of a series for TV, entitled *Carnivàle*, twenty-four episodes situated in the Dust Bowl during the meager years of the nineteen-thirties.[3] Perhaps you have watched it. The series depicts the struggle between light and dark, good and evil,

2. Lévi-Strauss, *Structural Anthropology*, 169–73.

3. *Carnivàle*, created by Daniel Knauf, two series, twelve episodes each. HBO 2004, 2006.

free will and inescapable fate. It tells a modern myth, set in two contexts, one a traveling carnival troupe, the other an evangelical revival community. The two main characters are a boy picked up by the carnival people after his mother died, and a charismatic pastor-preacher. The story is too complicated to re-tell here, but there is one aspect that really struck me. There is a persistent play with inversions, constantly urging the viewer to adapt her or his u-asses. Whereas the carnival initially appears as the place where everything that God has forbidden takes place, and the pastor's community is presented as God-fearing, in the end this duality is inverted, even though the picture is not so black-white as to make the inversion total. The carnival boy reveals himself to be a healing savior, whereas the pastor is exposed as the devil's servant. I am reminded of this because *Carnivàle* perforates the borders of the common repertoires of u-asses. And that is what I have been looking to do in this book.

I do hope you recognize this. Whether you see yourself as being religious or secular, or perhaps in-between, I would urge you to use your ability to play with what others consider fixed positions. Make it your habit to look for possible inversions. However, do not make this your daily bread. You need some order as well, getting answers, even if provisional, to the basic questions of human life, in relation to life and death, good and evil, true and false, beautiful and unsightly, as well as authentic and problematic identities. Adopting the playful perspective is not so much a matter of abandoning convictions, but of viewing them in a different way. Hopefully the context in which you experience your worldview is run by a leadership, if any, of the subservient type. Use that climate to find the game that suits you, old or new. Play it, let yourself be absorbed in it, but be critical of it from time to time. If you are religious, use ritual occasions, like meditation, pilgrimage, fasting or retreat, to revise your repertoire. If you are secular, you may wish to reread the books that inspired you, and see whether they still convince you. Don't make yourself dependent on other people's answers to the basic questions.

You might experiment with a position in the margin, from where you can observe what happens in the center, and yet also keep an eye on the answers given elsewhere. Or, perhaps better still, you could venture into the center, experimenting with forms of leadership that put an end to self-serving forms of power. I do hope you will seek to keep the institutional presence minimal. When introducing change into your life, you may consider applying the lesson from Congo that I referred to in chapter six.

You would then have to find an effective mode of participation, the right symbolic dramatization, and a sensible phasing-in. As far as human costs and benefits are concerned, please seek to keep the costs minimal. Feel challenged to reconsider convictions that are marked by the symbolism of self-serving power. If you are religious, remember that the divine name can be used for self-serving purposes. Be careful if somebody says "Thus speaks the Lord." Try to see your worldview, whether religious or secular, from within its social and cultural context. If you are part of the center, seek the margin from time to time, to look at yourself from a distance, and laugh at the seriousness of your u-asses. Yet, do not abandon them easily, but invest in their maintenance, revising them every 10,000 miles, and replacing what is worn out.

Your attitude could have compassion as its leading value. Thus you might seek to understand how people formulate their answers to the basic questions, using the tools that the human animal has at her (or his) disposal, including a number of nasty shortcomings. You would be aware of the impossibility of finding the perfect answer or the flawless formulation. You would also bear in mind that the human animal's brains make her into a contortionist, who has difficulty in combining the opposing tendencies of the overwhelming aggregate and the controlled detail. It may be helpful to consider that human animals are skilled both in meaning-making and in restraining creativity. Try your hand at accepting that contrasting opinions can both be true. Enjoy the moment of play more than the conviction. Compassion may help you to find the right form of subservient power. You will discover that leaders are illusion-consuming animals as well.

It will be difficult to find your position on the spectrum between power and play. I have some recommendations and suggestions for you. Do not think that you can do without power, but do not let seriousness overtake play. Do not channel the wild river, and yet prevent play from getting out of control. If Lady Play needs to be emancipated from Lord Power, support her. If Lord Power is unable to make Lady Play happy, support him. Wake up when you start applying routines. Let not the system become hallowed. Keep space available for wild reflection, even when tamed to a ritualized form. Accept that a minimal degree of order demands a few borders, but prevent them from becoming eternal. Take an ironic position, without using the wink too often. Play your game, but do it in a serious, authentic, and convincing manner.

It would be good if you could let yourself be challenged regularly by views that you do not directly identify as yours. Just climb the wall and enjoy the view. Imagine life on the other side. Play the game of opposites, if only to know how it feels and to understand its u-asses. Perhaps a course in cultural anthropology would be a good idea. Reading novels that describe inversions of convictions provide pleasant experiences, especially those stories containing a conversion of views situated in a multi-cultural setting. My personal favorite examples are Margaret Craven's *I Heard the Owl Call My Name*[4] and Shûsaku Endô's *Silence*.[5] Craven describes the transformation of an Anglican priest going to work among Amerindians on the Canadian West Coast, and Endô tells the story of a Catholic priest in seventeenth-century Japan who adopts the Japanese perspective.

It may be a good idea to evaluate modernization for its risks and opportunities. Please do not reject or embrace modernization completely. Occupy the space it provides for free meaning-making, but distrust the ready-made, universally valid, commercial worldview recipes it thrusts upon you. Be aware of all the changes that modernization has brought in producing modern society and seek to discover the challenges these changes represent to your repertoire, both religious and secular. You may want to weigh up these changes to see what they mean in terms of quality of life and freedom of meaning-making. Always calculate the human cost. If you come from a bordering background, find a playful way to deal with religious diversity, the God Debate, the role of power and the global problems. If your worldview is secular, you may find it useful to spend time examining your u-asses on these topics. See what your worldview's role is in causing and solving the four global problems of poverty, violence, pollution, and conflict.

Consider the opportunities that your life as a professional or as a volunteer offers. If you identify with it, feel free to translate this book to your specific context. You may discover how in your concrete situation power and play are related. See whether their arduous marriage can be made more cheerful and durable. Find your place on the spectrum between structure and challenge. It would be wonderful if you could map the u-asses of your setting. In doing so you may become aware of the schema repertoire of your worldview. You may feel the need to develop a repertoire for your own

4. Craven, *I Heard the Owl Call My Name*.
5. Endô, *Silence*.

playful third path. Make yourself known to be playful, but play that role seriously.

A final inversion that helps to make a playful worldview the most powerful: Let not prose hide poetry. Find how more can be said with less. Speak when you think you have something to say, remain silent and listen when the words do not come. Discover the resemblance between poetry and worldview, both being forms of "whole thinking."

Yours, with playful greetings,

André

Listen! I will be honest with you,

I do not offer the old smooth prizes, but offer rough new prizes,

These are the days that must happen to you:

You shall not heap up what is call'd riches,

You shall scatter with lavish hand all that you earn or achieve,

You but arrive at the city to which you were destin'd, you hardly settle yourself to satisfaction before you are call'd by an irresistible call to depart,

You shall be treated to the ironical smiles and mockings of those who remain behind you,

What beckonings of love you receive you shall only answer with passionate kisses of parting,

You shall not allow the hold of those who spread their reach'd hands toward you.

— *Walt Whitman*

Bibliography

Alexander, Franz. "A Contribution to the Theory of Play." *Psychoanalytical Quarterly* 27 (1958) 175–93.

Almond, Gabriel A., et al. *Strong Religion: The Rise of Fundamentalisms Around the World*. Chicago: The University of Chicago Press, 2003.

Alves, Rubem. *The Poet, the Warrior, the Prophet*. London: SCM, 2002.

Anderson, Allan, et al. *Studying Global Pentecostalism: Theories and Methods*. Berkeley: University of California Press, 2010.

Antelme, Robert. *The Human Race*. Marlboro, VT: Marlboro, 1992.

Antoun, Richard T. *Understanding Fundamentalism: Christian, Islamic and Jewish Movements*. Walnut Creek, CA: Rowman & Littlefield, 2008.

Appelros, Erica. *God in the Act of Reference: Debating Religious Realism and Non-Realism* Farnham, UK: Ashgate, 2002.

————. "Playing and Believing." *Studia Theologica* 55.1 (2001) 23–40.

Armstrong, Karen. *The Great Transformation: The Beginning of Our Religious Traditions*. New York: Knopf, 2006.

Baal, J. van. *Symbols for Communication: An Introduction to the Anthropological Study of Religion*. Assen: Van Gorcum, 1971.

Barthes, Roland. *Oeuvres Complètes, Tome V: Livres Textes, Entretiens 1977-1980*. Paris: Seuil, 2002.

Bateson, Gregory. "A Theory of Play and Fantasy." In *Steps to an Ecology of Mind: Collected Essays in Anthropology, Psychiatry, Evolution and Epistemology*, 150–66. St. Albans, UK: Paladin, 1973.

Bell, Catherine. *Ritual Theory, Ritual Practice*. Oxford: Oxford University Press, 1992.

Bellah, Robert N. *Religion in Human Evolution: From the Paleolithic to the Axial Age*. Cambridge: Belknap, 2011.

Berger, Peter, et al. *Religious America, Secular Europe? A Theme and Variations*. Aldershot, UK: Ashgate, 2008.

Berlin, Isaiah. *The Hedgehog and the Fox: An Essay on Tolstoy's View of History*. London: Weidenfeld and Nicholson, 1953.

Berry, Philippa, and Andrew Wernick. *Shadow of Spirit: Postmodernism and Religion*. London: Routledge, 1992.

Blake, William. *Poems*. Selected and Introduced by Patti Smith. London: Vintage, 2007.

Bloch, Maurice. "Language, Anthropology and Cognitive Science." *Man* 26 (1991) 183–98.

Borg, Meerten ter, and Jan Willem van Henten. *Powers: Religion as a Social and Spiritual Force*. New York: Fordham University Press, 2010.

Caillois, Roger. "The Definition of Play, The Classification of Games." In *The Game Design Reader: A Rules of Play Anthology*, edited by Katie Salen and Eric Zimmerman, 122–55. Cambridge: MIT, 2006.

———. *Man, Play, and Games*. New York: Schocken, 1979.

Casanova, José. *Public Religions in the Modern World*. Chicago: Chicago University Press, 1994.

Clarke, Peter B. *The Oxford Handbook of the Sociology of Religion*. Oxford: Oxford University Press, 2009.

Clarke, Peter B., and Peter Byrne. *Religion Defined and Explained*. London: Collier-Macmillan and St. Martin's Press, 1993.

Cox, Harvey. *Feast of Fools*. Cambridge: Harvard University Press, 1969.

Cox, James L. *An Introduction to the Phenomenology of Religion*. London: Continuum, 2010.

Craven, Margaret. *I Heard the Owl Call My Name*. London: Picador, 1974.

Cunningham, Graham. *Religion and Magic: Approaches and Theories*. Edinburgh: Edinburgh University Press, 1999.

D'Andrade, Roy. *The Development of Cognitive Anthropology*. Cambridge: Cambridge University Press, 1995.

Davie, Grace, et al. *Europe: The Exceptional Case: Parameters of Faith in the Modern World*. London: Darton, Longman and Todd, 2002.

———. *Predicting Religion: Christian, Secular and Alternative Futures*. Aldershot, UK: Ashgate, 2003.

———. *Religion in Britain since 1945: Believing without Belonging*. Oxford: Blackwell, 1994.

———. *The Sociology of Religion*. Los Angeles: SAGE, 2013.

Dawkins, Richard. *The God Delusion*. London: Black Swan, 2007.

Dickinson, Emily. *The Selected Poems of Emily Dickinson*. Ware, UK: Wordsworth Editions, 1994.

Dobbelaere, Karel. "The Meaning and Scope of Secularization." In *The Oxford Handbook of the Sociology of Religion*, edited by Peter B. Clarke, 599–615. Oxford: Oxford University Press, 2009.

Docherty, Thomas. *Postmodernism: A Reader*. New York: Harvester Wheatsheaf, 1993.

Douglas, Mary. *Natural Symbols: Explorations in Cosmology*. New York: Vintage, 1970.

Droogers, André. *The Dangerous Journey: Symbolic Aspects of Boys' Initiation among the Wagenia of Kisangani, Zaire*. The Hague: Mouton/De Gruyter, 1980.

———. "Defining Religion: A Social Science Approach." In *The Oxford Handbook of the Sociology of Religion*, edited by Peter B. Clarke, 263–79. Oxford: Oxford University Press, 2009.

———. "From Waste-making to Recycling: A Plea for an Eclectic Use of Models in the Study of Religious Change." In *Theoretical Explorations in African Religion,* edited by Wim van Binsbergen and Matthew Schoffeleers, 101–37. London: KPI, 1985.

———. "Methodological Ludism: Beyond Religionism and Reductionism." In *Conflicts in Social Science,* edited by Anton van Harskamp, 44–67. London: Routledge, 1996.

———. *Play and Power in Religion: Collected Essays*. Berlin: De Gruyter, 2012.

———. "The Recovery of Perverted Religion: Internal Power Processes and the Vicissitudes of Religious Experience." In *Powers: Religion as a Social and Spiritual*

Force, edited by Meerten ter Borg and Jan Willem van Henten, 23–38. New York: Fordham University Press, 2010.

———. "Symbols of Marginality in the Biographies of Religious and Secular Innovators: A Comparative Study of the Lives of Jesus, Waldes, Booth, Kimbangu, Buddha, Mohammed and Marx." *Numen* 27.1 (1980) 105–21. Reprinted in *Play and Power in Religion: Collected Essays*, 35–50. Berlin: De Gruyter, 2012.

———. "Towards the Concerned Study of Religion: Exploring the Double Power-play Disparity." *Religion, a Journal of Religion and Religions* 40.4 (2010) 227–38.

Droogers, André, and Anton van Harskamp. *Methods for the Study of Religious Change: From Religious Studies to Worldview Studies*. Sheffield, UK: Equinox, 2014.

Dufour, Dany-Robert. *Le Divin Marché: La révolution culturelle libérale*. Paris: Denoël, 2007.

———. *On achève bien les hommes: De quelques conséquences actuelles et futures de la mort de Dieu*. Paris: Denoël, 2005.

Durkheim, Emile. *The Elementary Forms of the Religious Life*. London: George Allen & Unwin, 1976.

Ehrmann, Jacques, et al. "Homo Ludens Revisited." *Yale French Studies* 41 (1968) 31–57.

Elliott, Anthony, and Charles Lemert. *The New Individualism: The Emotional Costs of Globalization*. London: Routledge, 2006.

Ellul, Jacques. *La subversion du christianisme*. Paris: Seuil, 1984. English translation: *The Subversion of Christianity*. Grand Rapids: Eerdmans, 1986.

Endô, Shûsaku. *Silence*. New York: Taplinger, 1980.

Fink, Eugen. *Spiel als Weltsymbol*. Stuttgart: Kohlhammer, 1960.

Geertz, Clifford. "Deep Play: Notes on the Balinese Cockfight." In *The Interpretation of Cultures*, 412–52. New York: Basic, 1973.

Gray, John. *Strawdogs: Thoughts on Humans and Other Animals*. London: Granta, 2002.

Guba, Egon G. *The Paradigm Dialog*. London: SAGE, 1990.

Heelas, Paul, and Linda Woodhead. *The Spiritual Revolution: Why Religion is Giving Way to Spirituality*. Oxford: Blackwell, 2005.

Hijmans, Ellen, and Adri Smaling. "Over de relatie tussen kwalitatief onderzoek en levensbeschouwing: Een inleiding," In *Kwalitatief onderzoek en levensbeschouwing*, 12–32. Amsterdam: Boom, 1997.

Hitchens, Christopher. *God is Not Great*. London: Atlantic, 2007.

———. *The Portable Atheist: Essential Readings for the Nonbeliever*. Philadelphia: Da Capo, 2007.

Houtman, Dick, et al. *Paradoxes of Individualization: Social Control and Social Conflict in Contemporary Modernity*. Farnham, UK: Ashgate, 2011.

Houtman, Dick, and Birgit Meyer. *Things: Religion and the Question of Materiality*. New York: Fordham University Press, 2012.

Huizer, Gerrit, and Bruce Mannheim. *The Politics of Anthropology: From Colonialism and Sexism toward a View from Below*. The Hague: Mouton, 1979.

Huizinga, Johan. *Homo Ludens: A Study of the Play-element in Culture*. Boston: Beacon, 1955.

Hunt, Stephen J. *Religion in Western Society*. New York: Palgrave, 2002.

Huntington, Samuel P. *The Clash of Civilizations and the Remaking of World Order*. London: Touchstone, 1998.

James, William. *The Varieties of Religious Experience: A Study in Human Nature*. New York: Mentor, 1958.

Jensen, Tim, and Mikael Rothstein. *Secular Theories on Religion: Current Perspectives.* Copenhagen: Museum Tusculanum, 2000.

Johannesen, Stanley. "Third-Generation Pentecostal Language: Continuity and Change in Collective Perceptions." In *Charismatic Christianity as a Global Culture*, edited by Karla Poewe, 176–99. Columbia, SC: University of South Carolina Press, 1994.

Kemp, Daren, and James R. Lewis. *Handbook of New Age.* Leiden: Brill, 2007.

Kinsley, David R. *The Divine Player: A Study of Krsna Lila.* Delhi: Motilal Banarsidass, 1979.

Kliever, Lonnie D. "Fictive Religion: Rhetoric and Play." *The Journal of the American Academy of Religion* 49 (1981) 657–69.

Knibbe, Kim, and André Droogers. "Methodological Ludism and the Academic Study of Religion." *Method and Theory in the Study of Religion* 23 (2011) 283–303.

Kuhn, Thomas S. *The Structure of Scientific Revolutions.* Chicago: University of Chicago Press, 1970.

Lawrence, Bruce B. "From Fundamentalism to Fundamentalisms: A Religious Ideology in Multiple Forms." In *Religion, Modernity and Postmodernity*, edited by Paul Heelas, 88–101. Oxford: Blackwell, 1998.

Lehmann, Arthur C., and James E. Myers. *Magic, Witchcraft, and Religion: An Anthropological Study of the Supernatural.* Mountain View, CA: Mayfield, 1989.

Lenoir, Frédéric. *Le Christ philosophe.* Paris: Plon, 2007.

Lévi-Strauss, Claude. *La pensée sauvage.* Paris: Plon, 1962. English translation: *The Savage Mind.* Chicago: University of Chicago Press, 1969.

———. *Structural Anthropology.* Garden City, NY: Anchor, Doubleday, 1967.

Márquez, Gabriel García. *Collected Stories.* New York: Harper Perennial Classics, 1999.

Marty, Martin E., and R. Scott Appleby. *Fundamentalisms Observed.* Chicago: University of Chicago Press, 1991.

McFague, Sally. *Metaphorical Theology.* London: SCM, 1983.

McGilchrist, Iain. *The Master and his Emissary: The Divided Brain and the Making of the Western World.* New Haven: Yale University Press, 2009.

Michael, David R., and Sandra L. Chen. *Serious Games: Games That Educate, Train and Inform.* Mason, OH: Course Technology, 2006.

Michelson, Bruce. "Deus Ludens: The Shaping of Mark Twain's Mysterious Stranger." *Novel: A Forum on Fiction* 14.1 (1980) 44–56.

Miller, David Leroy. *Gods and Games: Toward a Theology of Play.* New York: World, 1970.

Müller, Markus. "Interview with René Girard." *Anthropoetics* 2.1 (1996). No pages. Online: www.anthropoetics.ucla.edu/ap0201/interv.htm.

Nemoianu, Virgil, and Robert Royal. *Play, Literature, Religion: Essays in Cultural Intertextuality.* Albany, NY: State University of New York Press, 1992.

Otto, Rudolf. *The Idea of the Holy.* London: Oxford University Press, 1936.

Pals, Daniel L. *Eight Theories of Religion.* Oxford: Oxford University Press, 2006.

Popper, Karl. *The Open Society and Its Enemies.* London: Routledge, 1999.

Pruyser, Paul W. *A Dynamic Psychology of Religion.* New York: Harper & Row, 1976.

———. *The Play of the Imagination: Toward a Psychoanalysis of Culture.* New York: International Universities Press, 1983.

Quintana, Mário. *Caderno H.* Porto Alegre, Brazil: Globo, 1983.

Rahner, Karl. *Theological Investigations, Vol. 14.* London: Darton, Longman and Todd, 1976.

Rappaport, Roy A. *Ritual and Religion in the Making of Humanity.* Cambridge: Cambridge University Press, 1999.

Reedijk, Rachel. *Roots and Routes: Identity Construction and the Jewish-Christian-Muslim Dialogue*. Amsterdam: Rodopi, 2010.

Rosenau, Pauline Marie. *Post-modernism and the Social Sciences: Insights, Inroads, and Intrusions*. Princeton: Princeton University Press, 1992.

Rue, Loyal. *Religion Is Not about God: How Spiritual Traditions Nurture Our Biological Nature and What to Expect When They Fail*. New Brunswick, NJ: Rutgers University Press, 2005.

Safranski, Rüdiger. *Das Böse oder das Drama der Freiheit*. München: Hanser, 1997.

Seiwert, Hubert. "Theory of Religion as Myth: On Loyal Rue, *Religion Is Not about God* (2005)." In *Contemporary Theories of Religion: A Critical Companion*, edited by Michael Stausberg, 224–41. London: Routledge, 2009.

Sexson, Lynda. *Ordinarily Sacred*. Charlottesville, VA: University Press of Virginia, 1992.

Shupe, Anson. "Religious Fundamentalism." In *The Oxford Handbook of the Sociology of Religion*, edited by Peter B. Clarke, 478–90. Oxford: Oxford University Press, 2009.

Slyke, James A. Van. *The Cognitive Science of Religion*. Farnham, UK: Ashgate, 2011.

Stausberg, Michael. *Contemporary Theories of Religion: A Critical Companion*. London: Routledge, 2009.

Strauss, Claudia, and Naomi Quinn. *A Cognitive Theory of Cultural Meaning*. Cambridge: Cambridge University Press, 1997.

Sutton-Smith, Brian. *The Ambiguity of Play*. Cambridge: Harvard University Press, 1997.

Synnott, Anthony. *The Body Social: Symbolism, Self, and Society*. London: Routledge, 1993.

Taylor, Charles. *A Secular Age*. Cambridge: Belknap, 2007.

Thrower, James. *Religion: The Classical Theories*. Edinburgh: Edinburgh University Press, 1999.

Trotter II, Robert T., and Jean J. Schensul. "Methods in Applied Anthropology." In *Handbook of Methods in Cultural Anthropology*, edited by Bernard H. Russell, 691–735. Walnut Creek, CA: AltaMira, 1998.

Turner, Victor W. *The Anthropology of Performance*. New York: PAJ, 1988.

———. *From Ritual to Theatre: The Human Seriousness of Play*. New York: PAJ, 1982.

———. *The Ritual Process: Structure and Anti-Structure*. Harmondsworth, UK: Penguin, 1974.

Turner, Victor W., and Edith Turner. *Image and Pilgrimage in Christian Culture*. New York: Columbia University Press, 1977.

Unamo, Miguel de. *Tragic Sense of Life*. Translated by J. E. Crawford Flitch. New York: Dover, 1954.

Vaihinger, Hans. *The Philosophy of "As If."* Translated by C. K. Ogden. London: Routledge and Kegan Paul, 1953.

Vidal, Gore. *Creation: A Novel*. New York: Random House, 1981.

Visala, Aku. *Naturalism, Theism and the Cognitive Study of Religion: Religion Explained?* Farnham, UK: Ashgate, 2011.

Vries, Hent de, *Religion: Beyond a Concept*. New York: Fordham University Press, 2008.

Whitehouse, Harvey, and James Laidlaw. *Religion, Anthropology, and Cognitive Science*. Durham, NC: Carolina Academic Press, 2007.

Whitman, Walt. *Leaves of Grass*. With an Introduction by Gay Wilson Allen. New York: Signet Classic, New American Library, 1958.

Williams, James G. *The Girard Reader*. New York: Crossroad, 1996.

Winnicott, D. W. *Playing and Reality*. London: Tavistock, 1971.

Notes to Poems

page 12: Whitman, *Leaves of Grass,* 215.

page 25: Whitman, *Leaves of Grass,* 307–8.

page 40: Online: http://en.wikipedia.org/wiki/
   When_I_have_Fears_that_I_may_Cease_to_Be.

page 70: Dickinson, *Selected Poems,* 19.

page 91: Dickinson, *Selected Poems*, 44.

page 119: Blake, *Poems*, 95.

page 148: Blake, *Poems,* 90.

page 160: Whitman, *Leaves of Grass,* 141.

GENERAL INDEX

aesthetic, 9, 17, 19, 47, 49, 58, 100
African Independent Churches, 36
agricultural revolution, 29
Alexander, Franz, 93
Almond, Gabriel A., 7
Alves, Rubem, 13, 34, 103, 105
Antelme, Robert, 55
antithetical, 11, 96
anthropology, anthropologist, 71,
    101, 127, 155, 158
Antoun, Richard T., 7
Appelros, Erica, 135
Argent, Angela, ix
Armstrong, Karen, 29
atheism, atheists, vii, 1, 4–6, 8, 10–11,
    44, 54, 125–30, 135, 138, 141,
    146, 150–51, 154–55
Axial Period, 29–30

Baal, J. van, 28, 111
Barthes, Roland, 85
Bateson, Gregory, 93
beauty, 13, 15, 18–19, 72, 100, 149
believers, vii, 1–6, 8–11, 17, 19–20,
    24, 36–38, 44–47, 50, 59–61,
    63–65, 75–76, 78–79, 81,
    84, 86–89, 92–94, 99–100,
    120–25, 128–32, 135, 137–44,
    147, 154
Bell, Catherine, 78
Bellah, Robert N., 28–29, 92
Berger, Peter, 7
Berlin, Isaiah, 103

Berry, Philippa, 46
Blake, William, 119, 148
Bloch, Maurice, 101
Boas, Franz, 155
body, 13–21, 24, 38, 48, 50, 52–53,
    65–66, 71–72, 89, 98
bordering, 1–11, 28, 37, 39, 41, 48,
    63–68, 75–79, 84, 87–90, 92–
    93, 100, 110, 113, 115, 118,
    120–29, 131–32, 134, 137–38,
    141–47, 149, 151–52, 156–58
    definition of bordering, 1, 151
Borg, Meerten ter, 146
brain, brain hemispheres, 27, 32–33,
    37, 40, 89, 101–3, 105–6,
    108–9, 111–12, 114–17, 122,
    126, 128–30, 133, 135–36,
    142, 144–45, 149–51, 153,
    157
Buddha, 15, 83
Buddhism, 29, 85–86
Byrne, Peter, 43

Caillois, Roger, 93–94
Carnivàle, 155–56
Casanova, José, 7
Catholic(ism), 78, 81, 158
Chen, Sandra L., 95
Christianity, 4, 29, 36, 49, 76–77, 80,
    85–87, 135
church, 58–59, 76, 78, 80, 133
Clarke, Peter B., 43
clash of civilizations 1, 122

compassion, 14, 80, 87, 135, 137, 157
conflict, 5, 11, 32–33, 44, 65, 67, 74,
    81, 86, 88, 121–22, 130, 137–
    39, 142, 145, 150, 158
connectionism, 101–2, 107–109
construct, constructivism, 1, 6,
    45–47, 54, 60–61, 97, 103,
    128, 137
consumerism, 32, 48, 67–68
conversion, 36, 79, 88, 116, 132,
    136–37, 140, 152, 158
Copernicus, 7
corporeal, *see* body
Cox, Harvey, 93, 135
Cox, James L., 37
Craven, Margaret, 158
creative, creativity, 3, 15, 20, 24, 74,
    96, 109, 111–12, 122, 124,
    134, 157
cult, 15, 17–18, 20–21, 36, 81, 83–84,
    94
culture, cultural, 2–3, 7, 21, 23, 27–
    31, 33–34, 37, 47, 53, 65, 67,
    76, 95, 101, 105–9, 111, 125,
    127, 130, 132, 135, 147, 150,
    153, 157–58
Cunningham, Graham, 43

D'Andrade, Roy, 101, 107–9
Darwin, Charles, 7, 130
Davie, Grace, 7, 133
Dawkins, Richard, vii, 4, 23
death, 13, 15–24, 36, 52, 54, 59, 65–
    66, 89, 96, 124, 149, 156
desert, 13, 15, 51, 65
devil, 37, 67, 156
devolution, 32, 39, 152
dialogue, *see* interreligious dialogue
Dickinson, Emily, 70, 91
discipline, disciplinary, 6, 17, 65, 122,
    128, 132, 151
discipline (academic), 11, 47, 58, 62,
    107, 131, 143–44
diversity, *see* religious diversity

divine, divinity, 5–6, 11, 15, 19, 37,
    42, 44, 51–58, 62, 66–67,
    75–81, 99, 116, 135, 138–41,
    148, 154–55, 157
Dobbelaere, Karel, 7
Docherty, Thomas, 46
domestication of wild reflection, 30,
    33–35, 39, 64, 69, 98, 101,
    113, 144, 150
Douglas, Mary, 66
Droogers, André, 8–9, 13, 15, 32, 44,
    46, 60, 62, 72, 95, 107, 124,
    143, 145
dualism, dualistic, duality, 1, 6, 28,
    59, 63, 67, 75, 95, 156
Durkheim, Émile, 54
dynamics, 20–21, 26, 58, 80, 84, 90,
    99, 113, 122, 151

eclectic, 56
Eddy, Mary Baker, 83
education, 10, 64, 95, 109, 140–42
Ehrmann, Jacques, 103
Elliott, Anthony, 45
Ellul, Jacques, 76
emotion, 2, 47, 89, 107, 136–37
Endô, Shûsaku, 158
Enlightenment, 50, 110, 113, 115,
    125, 150
epistemological, 9, 17, 19, 47, 100
Esteban, 14–18, 20–21, 23–24, 26,
    28, 35, 38, 71–73, 82–84, 88,
    99, 154
ethic(al), 9, 17, 19, 47, 58, 100, 135
evil, 33, 48, 55–56, 62, 67, 100, 155
evolution(ism), 27, 32–33, 102, 130
exclusive religion, religious
    exclusivity, 1, 4, 8–9, 37, 54,
    63–67, 77, 70, 84, 88, 113,
    121–22, 126–27, 139, 149,
    151–52
existential questions, *see* ultimate
    questions
experience, 2, 6–7, 15–18, 20, 22–24,
    30, 41, 45, 47–48, 50–56, 59–

61, 63, 66–68, 72–73, 75–77,
    79–80, 82–87, 89, 98–99,
    101–4, 108–16, 121–22, 131,
    134–37, 140, 142–43, 154,
    156, 158
explanation, explanatory, 7–8, 42–44,
    47, 59–63, 114, 116, 143

fiction(al), vii, 14–15, 20, 31, 36, 109,
    128
Fink, Eugen, 93
fragmentation, 7, 53, 104, 106, 112
functional(ism), 42–44, 47, 58, 60, 62,
    110, 112, 115–17, 127
functional definition of religion,
    42–44, 60
fundamentalism, 2–4, 7, 113, 126,
    142

Galileo, 7
game, 8, 11, 16, 19, 23, 32, 46, 52, 86,
    94–95, 97, 123–27, 129, 131,
    137, 140–141, 143, 153–58
Geertz, Clifford, 93
Girard, René, 81–82, 115, 117
global problems, vii, 3, 6, 9–10,
    31–32, 56, 63, 67, 120, 137,
    139–40, 142–46, 150–51, 158
global village, 26, 31
globalization, 6–7, 89, 109, 121, 144,
    151
God, gods, 20, 37–38, 49, 51, 53–54,
    56–57, 65–66, 75–76, 80, 99,
    125–26, 128, 130–33, 135,
    141, 148, 154, 156
    God Debate, 3, 5–6, 9–11, 39, 54,
        63, 120, 125, 128, 130, 133,
        141, 158
Gray, John, 27
Guba, Egon G., 46, 127

Heelas, Paul, 53
Harskamp, Anton van, 9, 143
Henten, Jan Willem van, 146

Hijmans, Ellen, 9
Hildegard von Bingen, 83
Hinduism, 29
Hirokazu Kore-eda, 22
Hitchens, Christopher, vii, 7, 23
holy, 42, 44, 58, 65, 72
holy scriptures, 77, 85, 137
holy war, 139
Homo Hierarchicus, 11
Homo Ludens, 11, 128, 131
Houtman, Dick, 44, 146
Huizer, Gerrit, 145
Huizinga, Johan, 92–95
human
    ability, capacity, 2, 5, 8–9, 20, 24,
        26–27, 29, 33–39, 43, 48–50,
        55–57, 60, 62, 68, 73, 77, 79,
        81–82, 85, 92, 95–98, 102,
        110, 112, 118, 121, 126, 144,
        146, 148, 152, 154, 156
    animal, 2, 26–29, 31, 33–35, 37,
        39, 41, 46–48, 50–55, 60,
        62–63, 66, 68–69, 82, 85, 87,
        92–93, 98, 101–2, 109–11,
        118, 121, 126, 129–30, 135,
        139, 144, 149–53, 155, 157
    condition, 10, 49, 61, 92, 101, 111
    cost, vii, 1, 3, 8–9, 30, 96, 120,
        122–25, 129–30, 135, 137,
        139, 143, 147, 151, 157–58
humanity, 6, 8, 10, 32, 56–57, 120,
    147
Hunt, Stephen J., 7
Huntington, Samuel P., 1, 122, 125,
    138

identity, 6, 9, 17–19, 21, 33, 43, 47,
    53, 58, 66–67, 92, 100, 122,
    138, 144, 149, 154
image, imagination, 3, 7, 13–14,
    18–19, 24, 30–31, 34–36, 38,
    43, 48–50, 52, 55–56, 63–64,
    68, 75–76, 80, 82, 84, 87, 89,
    103, 107, 111–12, 114, 122,
    127–28, 130, 135, 140, 148,
    154, 158

individual, individualism,
  individualization, 5, 9, 28, 30,
  33, 35–36, 53–54, 56–57, 66,
  73, 89, 100, 106, 116–17, 124,
  136–37, 151, 154
industrialization, 30, 105
insiders, 2, 6, 44, 65, 67
interreligious dialogue, 13, 50, 129,
  132, 145
Islam, 29, 36, 86, 121

James, William, 45
Jasper, Karl, 29
Jensen, Tim, 43
Jesus, 15, 21, 76, 79, 83, 88, 91
Johannesen, Stanley, 113
Judaism, 29, 49

Kemp, Daren, 136
Kinsley, David R., 93
Kliever, Lonnie D., 93
Knibbe, Kim, 145
Kuhn, Thomas S., 126

Laidlaw, James, 47, 127
language, 27, 47, 57, 77, 79–80, 85,
  89, 97, 103–4, 107, 109, 113,
  130
Lawrence, Bruce B., 7
leaders, leadership, vii, 2, 5–6, 10, 54,
  58, 67, 73, 77, 80, 84, 86–89,
  92, 99–100, 111, 116, 122–23,
  133–34, 137–38, 140, 142–43,
  151, 154, 156–57
Lehmann, Arthur C., 116
Lemert, Charles, 35
Lenoir, Frédéric, 76
Lévi-Strauss, Claude, 34, 155
Lewis, James R., 136
Luther, Martin, 88, 114

magic, 40, 57, 115–16
magical realism, 13, 20

Mannheim, Bruce, 145
margin(al), 15–20, 24, 38, 65, 78–80,
  82–84, 87–89, 96, 98–99,
  112–13, 127, 134–35, 142,
  150–51, 156–57
market, 31–32, 56–57, 67, 124, 128,
  154
Márquez, Gabriel García, 10, 13–16,
  18–19, 21, 24, 36, 38, 71, 82,
  87–88, 141, 154
Marty, Martin E., 7
McFague, Sally, 55
McPherson, Aimee Simple, 83
McGilchrist, Iain, 28, 48, 80, 101–7,
  110–18, 130–32, 134, 136–37,
  142, 144–45
meaning-making (see also
  signification), 1–2, 6–7, 9,
  17–18, 21, 24, 27–39, 43, 46–
  48, 50, 53, 55–56, 58, 60–63,
  66, 74, 81–82, 85–87, 92,
  96–102, 109–11, 118, 121–24,
  126, 129–30, 132–34, 136,
  138, 141, 144, 147, 149–53,
  157–58
  definition, 2
mechanistic perspective, 106, 112,
  116–17
metaphor, 15, 27, 51, 55–58, 60–61,
  64–66, 68, 75–76, 80–81, 102,
  104–5, 108, 110, 114–17, 131,
  135, 154
methodological, 46–47, 145
  agnosticism, 146
  atheism, 146
  ludism, 46, 145–46
  theism, 146
Meyer, Birgit, 146
Michael, David R., 95
Michelson, Bruce, 131
Miller, David Leroy, 93, 135
modernization, 1, 3, 7, 24, 29–33,
  36, 39, 45, 50, 55, 57, 66–67,
  100–102, 105, 125, 129–30,
  133, 142, 149–52, 154, 158
Mohammed, 79, 83

moral(s), 3, 9, 17, 19–20, 53–56, 67, 127, 138, 149, 153
Moses, 79
Müller, Markus, 82
music, 48, 56–57, 67, 83, 93, 95, 108, 128
Myers, James E., 116
myth, 14–15, 19, 37, 43, 47, 56, 64, 80–81, 103, 117, 139, 156

naturalist theories of religion, 44–45, 48, 145–46
nature, 21, 48, 51–52, 57, 59, 65, 100, 139
Nemoianu, Virgil, 93
neoteny, 28–29, 33, 82
New Age, 36, 136

ontological, 9, 19, 47, 58, 100
Otto, Rudolf, 45
outsiders, see insiders

Pals, Daniel L., 43
paradigm(atic), 48, 57, 127, 129, 131, 154
paradox(ical), 7, 17, 30, 32, 35, 37–38, 50, 60, 77, 81, 86–87, 113, 144
Pentecostalism, 36, 136
pilgrimage, 15, 71–72, 156
play, playfulness, vii–viii, 4, 8–11, 13, 16–17, 19, 23–24, 26–27, 29, 31–39, 41, 45–50, 52, 54, 57, 60–64, 68–69, 71, 86, 88, 90, 92–103, 107, 110–13, 116, 118–33, 135, 137–47, 149–59
    definition of play, 8, 9, 93–95, 103, 112, 146
    playful religion, see religion
poems, poetry, vii, 11, 21, 58, 82, 89, 102, 104, 132, 159
political, politicians, politics, 1, 28–30, 34–35, 51, 54, 72, 82–83, 95–96, 105, 122, 136, 146

pollution, 5, 56, 67, 120, 137, 139, 142, 145, 150
Popper, Karl, 96
postmodernism, 46
power, powerful, vii–viii, 3–6, 8–11, 15, 19–20, 33–37, 40, 48–54, 56, 59, 61–64, 68–69, 71, 73–90, 92–93, 95–100, 102, 104–7, 110–13, 115–18, 120, 122, 124, 126, 128–29, 131–47, 149–53, 155–59
    abuse, 10, 76, 135
    definition of power 4–5, 73–75, 78
    game, 8, 95, 97
    interests vii, 74, 85, 88, 97, 100, 112, 122, 139
    mechanisms vii, 3, 9, 33, 37, 63, 84, 88, 122, 124, 126, 128, 150
    self-serving, 54, 74–84, 86–90, 92, 96, 99, 111–12, 116–17, 128–29, 131, 133–42, 144–45, 150–51, 156–57
    subservient, 34, 74–77, 80, 82–84, 86–90, 92, 96, 99, 11, 117, 129, 133–37, 139–42, 144–45, 150, 156–57
poverty, 5, 56, 88, 120, 137–38, 142, 145, 150, 158
pre-modern, 7, 14, 31–32, 66, 125
Presbyterian, 78
proselytism, 36
Protestant(ism), 3, 78, 86
Pruyser, Paul W., 93, 95

Quakers, 50, 78
Quinn, Naomi, 101, 107–8
Quintana, Mário, 85

Rahner, Karl, 4
Rappaport, Roy A., 47
rational, 2, 7–8, 23, 34, 89, 94, 104, 106, 127, 129, 134, 136, 142, 153
Reedijk, Rachel, 3

reflection, 7, 9, 17–18, 20, 26, 33, 35,
    41, 48–50, 53, 60–61, 64, 66,
    69, 73, 81, 84, 89, 110–11,
    114, 121, 130, 149, 155, 157
Reformation, 78, 86, 114–15, 136,
    143
religion, religious, *passim*
    religion and global problems, vii,
        5, 9–10, 63, 67, 137, 139–46,
        150–51, 158
    criticism of religion, 1–3, 6, 10,
        52, 54, 88–89, 138
    definition of religion, 42–44, 60
    religious diversity, 2, 3–6, 8–10,
        27, 30,32, 34–39, 43, 58–59,
        63, 109, 112, 120–23, 125,
        139–41, 158
    religious education, 10, 140–143
    founders, vii, 15, 75
    religious game, 11, 46, 86, 124–
        25, 137, 140–41, 143, 154–58
    religious leaders, vii, 2, 5–6, 10,
        54, 58, 67, 73, 77, 80, 84,
        86–89, 92, 99–100, 111, 116,
        122–23, 133–34, 137–38, 140,
        142–43, 151, 154, 156–57
    religious movements, 15, 19, 36,
        85–86, 112–13
    religion at play, playful religion,
        vii-viii, 4, 8–11, 17, 23–24, 27,
        29, 32, 36–37, 39, 41, 45–46,
        48–49, 60–64, 68, 86, 90,
        96–97, 99–101, 103, 112–13,
        116, 118, 120–26, 128, 130,
        132–33, 135–44, 146–47,
        149–52, 154–56, 158
    science and religion, 41, 44, 126,
        129, 144–45,
    theory of religion, 10–11, 39,
        41–44, 46–48, 60–62, 64, 68,
        82, 98, 115–17
    religious virtuoso, 49, 79–80,
        83–84, 86, 111, 135
religion at play, *see* religion
Religious Studies, vii, 10–11, 37, 46,
    92, 115–16, 120–27, 143–47

ritual, 2, 16–17, 19–21, 32, 36–37, 43,
    47, 58, 64–65, 67, 77–79, 81–
    82, 85, 89, 94, 108, 110–12,
    114, 122–24, 156–57
Rosenau, Pauline Marie, 46
Rothstein, Mikael, 43
Royal, Robert, 93
Rue, Loyal, 47

sacred, 3, 19, 38, 42, 44–45, 47, 49–
    51, 58–62, 64–65, 68, 74–77,
    79–82, 84–85, 87, 98–99, 125,
    133, 135, 142, 146, 154
Safranski, Rüdiger, 27
salvation, 4, 7, 15, 17, 47, 80, 136
schema, schema repertoire, 107–16,
    123, 125, 130, 132–34, 151,
    158
Schensul, Jean J., 145
Schouten, Ronald, 23
secular, 4, 10, 36, 44–45, 54, 61–62,
    75, 77–80, 86, 88, 99–100,
    123, 127, 134, 139, 145, 152–
    53, 156–58
secularization, 7, 57, 133, 152
Seiwert, Hubert, 47
self, 28, 31, 48, 53–54, 121, 154
self-serving power, *see* power
Sexson, Lynda, 85
Shupe, Anson, 3, 7
signification (*see also* meaning-
    making), 24, 31, 33–34,
    36–37, 48, 53, 98, 112
Slyke, James A. van, 47
Smaling, Adri, 9
Smith, Joseph, 83
sociology, sociological, 4, 80, 110
spiritual, 42, 53, 84, 102
Stausberg, Michael, 43–47
Strauss, Claudia, 101, 107–8
Study of Religion, *see* Religious
    Studies
subservient power, *see* power
substantial definition of religion, 42,
    44, 60, 62, 133

sustainable, sustainability, vii, 10, 120, 135, 138, 147
Sutton-Smith, Brian, 93
symbols, symbolism, 9, 15–21, 23–24, 37–38, 40, 43–44, 49–51, 55, 57, 62, 65, 72, 75, 80, 82, 85–86, 88, 99, 117, 123–24, 126–27, 131, 135, 143, 154, 157
syncretism, 11, 36, 89
Synnott, Anthony, 66

Taylor, Charles, 2
terrorism, 1, 31, 76, 121
theology, theological, 58–59, 80–81, 108, 110, 135–36, 140
theory, *see* religion
Thrower, James, 43–45
transcendence, transcendental, 42, 44–45, 54, 58, 65, 67–68, 75, 111, 129, 131, 145–46
transcendentalist theories of religion, 44, 145–46
tribal religion(s), 19, 36, 99–100
Trotter II, Robert T., 145
truth, 4, 8, 19, 61, 85, 91, 99, 107, 113, 125, 130, 149, 154
Turner, Victor W., 8, 15, 79, 92–93, 95, 132
Turner, Edith, 15

u-ass, unproven assumption, 152–58
ultimate (existential) questions, 9, 15, 17, 19–20, 26, 42, 49, 53, 58, 61, 63, 68, 83, 132
Unamo, Miguel de, 106
utopian, 8, 132, 147

Vaihinger, Hans, 131
Veen, Herman van, 22–23
Vidal, Gore, 29
violence 1, 5, 32, 56, 65, 67, 120–21, 124, 134, 137, 139, 145, 150, 158
Visala, Aku, 47
Vries, Hent de, 146

walls, 6–8, 112
wholes (greater, bigger, larger, uncontrollable), 28, 41, 48–49, 54, 59–61, 63, 66, 68, 75, 81, 98, 111–14, 116–17, 122, 130, 135, 140, 149, 151, 154
Wernick, Andrew, 46
Whitehouse, Harvey, 47, 127
Whitman, Walt, 12, 25, 160
Williams, James G., 81
Winnicott, D. W., 93
Woodhead, Linda, 53
world religions, 19, 29, 36, 86, 100
worldview, 1, 3–4, 7–11, 21, 26, 35–36, 42, 45, 52, 59, 66–67, 81–82, 100, 121–22, 125, 127, 129 131–32, 138, 145, 147, 149, 151–52, 156–59, 151–52, 156–59

Zen, 50, 89
Zoutewelle, Ineke, ix

www.ingramcontent.com/pod-product-compliance
Lightning Source LLC
Chambersburg PA
CBHW020333100426
42812CB00029B/3113/J